Middle Mania

Imaginative Theater Projects
for Middle School Actors

A Smith and Kraus Book
Published by Smith and Kraus, Inc.
177 Lyme Road, Hanover, NH 03755

First Edition: November 2001
10 9 8 7 6 5 4 3 2 1

Cover and Text Design by
Julia Hill Gignoux, Freedom Hill Design

Library of Congress Cataloguing-In-Publication Data
Johnson, Maureen Brady.
Middle mania : imaginative theater projects for middle school actors /
by Maureen Brady Johnson. —1st ed.
p. cm. — (Young actors series)
ISBN 1-57525-254-6
1. Improvisation (Acting) 2. Acting. 3. Puppet theater. 4. Acting—Study
and teaching (Middle school) I. Title. II. Series.
PN2071.I5 J628 2001
792'.028—dc21
2001054942

Middle Mania

Imaginative Theater Projects for Middle School Actors

by Maureen Brady Johnson

YOUNG ACTORS SERIES

A Smith and Kraus Book

Contents

DEDICATION

To My Husband, Mark
My Children: Erin, Allison, Juliet, and Sean
My parents, my family, my friends, my students,
and my teachers
Who never stopped believing in me.

ACKNOWLEDGMENTS

To all the people at Smith and Kraus for their support;

To the administrators and teachers at Lake Ridge Academy for their encouragement;

To all of my students for their willingness to try new things;

To the Educational Theatre Association and especially Jim Palmarini, the editor of *Teaching Theatre,* for giving me the opportunities to share my ideas;

To Matt Vanek for his help in the development of the Mask/Movement and Giant Puppet projects;

To Mary Fournier Bill who started me on this wondrous journey in theater.

Introduction

This book is written for all those theater teachers who spend a good part of their summer sifting through piles of bad plays in a quest for the perfect production to do with middle school students. This book gives you several creative alternatives that are "drama healthy" for your kids.

A limited diet of play productions in a drama class is like a diet of fast food: It gets repetitive, tiresome, and it's not good for you. At its worst, it can also be creatively dulling—turning kids off to drama for a long time. With a curriculum limited to play performances, students quickly realize that there is a hierarchy in place and the question, "Who has the lead?" works against community building.

A "drama healthy" curriculum provides every student with a chance to get involved. It gives the shy student a chance to build self-confidence. It also challenges boisterous students and stretches their imaginations. Students get excited about the possibilities that drama gives them. These projects build community much like a healthy diet builds strong bodies.

When I first began teaching middle school, I invented my own curriculum. I wanted to keep the kids safe onstage, that is, feeling confident enough to risk onstage. I taught sixth, seventh, and eighth grades. Each grade level was divided into two sections, and I met with each section twice a week for forty minutes. The sixth grade curriculum used a variety of projects that kept a performer hidden onstage by using puppets, masks, radio plays, and so on. The seventh grade took the students into units that emphasized working together as a group. After developing a mind set for a dramatic community, the eighth grade worked on production, playwriting, a mini-musical, and improvisational games.

I found that this approach to drama in middle school helped students develop at their own pace. It gave even the shyest child a chance and promoted community building at a time when much was working against this concept. Performance is used as a final product, but the projects challenge the creativity and imagination in a different way than a scripted play can. And I hardly ever hear, "Who has the lead?" because this is drama in which every student gets a chance to shine.

—Maureen Brady Johnson

The Chapters in a Nutshell

Chapter One: B.O.P. (Bag Of Puppets)
Grades 6 and 7

The "B.O.P." project began when I wondered what a group of kids would do with a random assortment of puppets in a paper bag. What if I told them they had to write a puppet show, using all the members in their group as puppeteers? As preparation for the B.O.P. assignment, I had a variety of mini-units like White Sock Monologue, a short study of puppet plays, and a preliminary writing exercise in which all of the students used the same puppet as the main character. The culminating activity was an original puppet show showing the relationships between all of the puppets in the paper bag.

Chapter Two: Mask/Movement
Grades 6 and 7

Mask making has always challenged the imagination. Adding music, storytelling, and movement enhances the creative experience. The lesson begins with a discussion of the history of mask making. I recommend using two videos. Then the students choose an emotion to portray in their mask, which they design and sketch. Constructing the masks comes next, using plaster-cast bandages, papier-mâché, and cardboard as materials. Some years I had the help of the Middle School art teacher. On the drama end of things, the students, through a series of improvisations, explore how to portray their emotion with their entire body. This is important because the mask covers the face, and the body will be used as the main communication tool in the performance. Then the students (in groups of five to eight) listen to instrumental music and write a story that incorporates their emotion. Next they practice their piece wearing their masks and present the final performance to the other groups in their class.

Chapter Three: Solving a Mystery: Clan Drama
Grade 7 and 8

Theater began thousands of years ago around campfires and in forests as ancient cultures tried to make sense of their worlds. This unit emphasizes the creation of a clan (groups of four or six) and the writing of a myth that explains a mystery of nature. It gives students a chance to discover the beginnings of theater, learn how to negotiate and cooperate, and have fun with costumes, music, and playwriting during the process.

Chapter Four: Giant Puppet Show
Grades 7 and 8

Using giant puppets to illustrate an original story is a larger-than-life experience. Designing the puppets and cutting them out of large pieces of cardboard saves time, but the students are capable of doing the preliminary work, too.

One of the ways to approach this unit is to design abstract shapes for the puppets. These shapes are cut out of large cardboard and shown to the students. During the following classes the students are introduced to pieces of instrumental music. Then they meet in small groups to write a story to accompany the music, keeping the shapes of the puppets in mind. It is a creative challenge to coordinate all of these elements. Then they decorate the puppet-shapes with found objects, paint, or markers. Rehearsal of the show, learning how to manipulate the giant puppets, and preparing for the final performance is exciting because every student is a puppeteer.

Another way to approach this unit is to take a children's story and make giant puppets to illustrate the story and act it out. Using music to introduce and close the performance adds to the tone of the show. We had a lot of fun making cardboard puppets for one of the stories because the kids did a "good" kid on one side and then flipped the cardboard puppet over to show the "bad" kid.

Chapter Five: "Musical Chairs"
Grades 7 and 8

I never liked musical chairs in grade school, so I took the premise of the game, twisted it around—adding original poetry, movement, and music—and came up with a great drama unit.

Every year our English classes generate wonderful poetry. I asked the kids to pick out their best pieces and bring them to drama class. We practiced reading the pieces with expression, enunciation, and projection. We divided the class into groups of five or seven and then we listened to some music with a lot of spunk. They were to invent a funky walk and practice it to the music. Then I set up three groups of chairs onstage (one group Stage Left, one group Stage Right, one group Center). We blocked the student groups to walk to a specific group of chairs onstage. When I stopped the music, one or two students from each group recited their poetry. The music started up again and they funky-walked to the next group of chairs. The music stopped and they read again. At the end of the performance, they funky-walked to exit the stage—performance-based musical chairs with no losers.

Chapter Six: Rock 'n' Roll Playwriting
Grade 8

This idea came to me as I was listening to an oldies station on the radio. They were playing a song about a teenage tragedy. I began to wonder what had happened before this song took place and what would happen after. So, I picked out some 50s songs, gave them to my students, and asked them to brainstorm (in groups of four to eight). I told them that they had to come up with a "before" and an "after" script in which the song was imbedded. They also had to lip-synch the song and then block it. We took some time out to study musical numbers from a variety of musicals, paying special attention to the way dialogue led into song. Everyone in the group was involved as they worked on getting the scene to hang together. When we presented these performances at the spring concert, they were the hit of the show!

This idea was the first lesson plan published by the Rock and Roll Hall of Fame and Museum in Cleveland.

Chapter Seven: Community Building Days
Grades 6, 7, and 8

In this chapter we explore how you can get an entire middle school focused on the arts for three full days and build community. The head of our Middle School wanted something different. For three years the school year had begun with three days of outdoor activities designed to bring the Middle School together to build community. He realized that the kids were getting tired of doing the same thing every year. I suggested using the arts as the unifying factor. With lots of cooperation and hard work from the faculty, the arts-based experience was a big success that culminated in eight giant puppet shows. The theme of the three days using art, music, and drama was "The World that We Can Create."

CHAPTER ONE

B. O. P. (Bag of Puppets)

GRADES SIX AND SEVEN

THE HISTORY BEHIND THE LESSON

I grew up on *Howdy Doody, Kukla, Fran, and Ollie,* and (I confess) watched *Sesame Street, The Muppet Show,* and *Fraggle Rock* with my children. I love puppets and what they can do for the shyest middle school student onstage. Puppets take on a life of their own. Students who will not say a word in a play develop the most lively and exciting characters when you give them a puppet.

From this came an idea: What if I were to give a random assortment of puppets in a large paper bag to a group of middle school students and ask them to produce a puppet show? They would have to show relationships between puppets as dissimilar as dogs, ladybugs, and fish. It would challenge their creativity and give them a chance to work as a group toward the goal of a polished script as everyone created a character and performed for their classmates. It seemed like a great idea, but first I needed to get some puppets.

BEFORE THE FIRST CLASS

The best kind of puppets are those that can be manipulated by hand. Students can put a lot of emotion and personality into their puppets when they can use their hands to work them.

I found a lot of puppets at garage sales and thrift stores, purchasing them for as little as a quarter. I asked our parent's association for puppet donations. They put a small article in the parent newsletter and the response was fantastic. Lots of people went through their closets and donated puppets their children had outgrown. We also had an all-school rummage sale, and I put the parents running the sale on "puppet alert"— as soon as a puppet was seen in a donation, it was put aside for our class. I soon had accumulated enough puppets for every student in a sixth grade class. I had two sections of sixth grade drama, each section numbering fifteen, and I used the same group of puppets for each section.

If you have a budget to purchase puppets, there are some outstanding companies that manufacture the most imaginative puppets. Folkmanis at *www.folkmanis.com* is an excellent resource, where I found an ant, a praying mantis, and an armadillo. Their web site also gives you a variety of tales to use with your puppets for possible connections with language arts and science teachers.

Please don't let the fact that you do not have the funds for buying a lot of puppets deter you from doing this lesson. Simple puppets can be made out of lunchbags. You could have classes make a set of puppets and then switch them. Approach the art teachers for some ideas for simple puppet construction using old pieces of junk or found objects.

You will also need some sturdy paper or plastic bags in which to store the puppets, and a notebook for the group secretary to record the script and its revisions.

Divide your class into groups before the unit begins. Put a variety of personalities together—some self-starters with some students who need a gentle push to concentrate and work. Use whatever grouping technique works for you. Sometimes friends work well together, sometimes you need to break them up. Part of the learning process with this unit is creating a complete and polished puppet show by working together as a group, compromising along the way.

I have had groups that work very well together—going way beyond the requirements of the project. I have had other groups struggle every step of the way. Many times the groups that struggle the most come up with the most imaginative and successful productions. The time and care you take when assembling the groups can make a big difference in both the journey and the performance.

I did not have a puppet theater for the final presentations. One year, I used a table covered with a large black cloth. I've also used a freestanding flat, 4' by 8', behind which a group can stand and manipulate their puppets. The puppet theater needs to fit the variety of heights that middle school students can be. One year I needed a box for one of the students to stand on so that his puppet could be seen, while another student had to duck down so the top of his head didn't show over the flat. Middle school students require flexibility and adaptability!

Some groups want elaborate sets for their shows, but keep the emphasis on character and story, not setting. Keep the set pieces simple and representational.

A syllabus to give them a break down of the classes and what would be required of the groups for each class period is very helpful. I find that this cuts down on wasted time. I spot-check the groups to give them a series of grades on the requirements achieved, but I will discuss that when we talk about assessment.

•　　•　　•

THE FIRST CLASS

I gather the class around me in a circle. Then I present them with a teaser of this unit—a short synopsis of the B.O.P. project along with a clear explanation of how they will be assessed. This creates a sense of anticipation and excitement about the process. It goes something like this...

> We are about to begin a journey into the world of puppetry. The final project involves an original puppet show presentation. You will receive a large bag of unrelated puppets—at least one for each of you. Your job will be to create interesting characters and to show relationships between these puppets. From these relationships, you will write a story with a lesson as its theme. Working in a group, you will have specific goals for each class period and the grade you receive will be based partially on the way you complete these goals. The rest of your grade will be based on the final performance. We will also be using peer and self-evaluation.
>
> Before we begin working on this project, you will have a chance to explore the world of puppetry. We will be examining and writing some short puppet plays to prepare for your final performance. You will be responsible for your own puppet monologue. All of these preparations will be averaged into your final grade. Does anyone have any questions?

At this point, most middle school students will want to know when they are going to get their bag of puppets. I reiterate the idea that we need to do some groundwork first to prepare them for the time when they get the Bag of Puppets.

Then I introduce them to my fish puppet. (The puppet you use to introduce the lesson should be unusual and imaginative...not necessarily expensive. You could even use a simple white sock on your hand!) I have a beautiful fish puppet from Folkmanis with shiny scales and the most unearthly blue color. My students literally gasp when I show it to them, it is so exotic and beautiful. I show them how to manipulate the puppet and explain how to treat the puppet, because the next step is to pass the puppet around the circle. This lesson in puppet care also clues them in on how to treat the puppets they will be receiving for their project. Reinforcing the proper treatment of the puppets several times during the unit is necessary for the long life of your puppets. Students need to understand the responsibility necessary to make the puppet project successful. Instilling this attitude is great prep work for future projects so that the students come to each dramatic experience with a growing understanding of the care and treatment of props and costumes. This approach spills over into their treatment of fellow performers, too.

For this introductory lesson, I use the book *Making Stories* by Irene Watts, published by Heinemann. It is a wonderful resource for storytelling. I look at the fish puppet and give it a name.

It looks like a Horace to me. What name would you give this fish?

The fish is passed around the circle and named. When the fish makes its way back to me, I begin a discussion asking to tell us something about their pet—an interesting happening, a funny story. I find, at this point, they volunteer all kinds of experiences. It's a wonderful way to get to know the students. Then I ask them what it might be like to have this fish as a pet and what kind of adventures the fish might have. For homework, they write a one-page adventure for the fish. I tell them that these stories will be graded, similar to a quiz grade, and that they should be original. Nothing should remind me of last night's TV episodes or the latest popular movie. Being creative and imaginative is worth a lot in my classroom.

•   •   •

SHARING THE STORIES (CLASSES 2 AND 3)

We begin seated in a circle, and students share their stories while holding the puppet. The kinds of things that present themselves for development and discussion are many and varied. A short list from which the teacher can choose follows:

1) The difficulty of puppet manipulation
2) The need for strong characterization
3) A story line with conflicting objectives to make the story more interesting
4) The importance of dialogue—making the story come alive
5) Showing vs. telling
6) How important a name can be in giving clues to a character

During this discussion, the teacher acts as a guide, asking questions that allow students to discover the elements of a successful puppet show.

Sometimes the sharing lasts for two class periods. At the end of these classes, we summarize all the important elements that we want to include in our puppet project, and I ask the students to bring in a plain white sock for the next class.

•   •   •

THE WHITE SOCK PUPPET MONOLOGUE (CLASSES 4–7)

This next set of exercises helps to develop a variety of skills. Here's the short list:

1) Transferring emotions to an inanimate object
2) Characterization
3) Using vocal ability to show the character of the puppet
4) Self-confidence as a puppeteer and a performer

Before this series of classes, I select some instrumental music that reflects a variety of emotions. Three or four pieces are sufficient. I also make up a long list of emotions. (A list of emotions can be found on page 124.)

We begin class in a circle and we talk about emotions—what they are, how people show emotion, and in particular, how performers show emotion using their faces, their bodies, their voices. We transfer this discussion to puppeteering and discuss how emotions are shown through an inanimate object. Then we come up with a list of emotions to add to my list.

Next, I play a piece of music and ask them what emotions the music inspires. Then I say, "This time when I play the music, move your hand (no puppets are used at this point, just the student's hand) in time to the music and try to show the emotions you're feeling in the movement of your hand."

I join in on this exercise because generally the kids feel self-conscious. It looks silly—so I look silly right alongside them. Risk taking lies at the heart of drama. It may take a while to get everyone involved in this hand-movement exercise, but eventually everyone will join in.

When the music stops, we discuss the emotions and the music. What did we see? What did we feel? I point out examples of the clear communication of an emotion.

"Kim. When you were moving your hand to that part of the music that was increasing in volume, the emotion you were portraying came across loud and clear!"

Then we each put a white sock onto our hand, and listen and move to the next selection of music. When the music stops, we discuss the problems and possibilities of using a white sock puppet. Here is a short list:

PROBLEMS
1) Not being able to see the expressiveness of the muscles in the hand
2) There's a limit to the fine movements that a person can do because of the sock on the hand

3) A student has to work harder to communicate an emotion.

POSSIBILITIES
1) You can use the sock material to create a new expressive "skin," i.e., making the mouth and eyes with thumb and knuckles.
2) With a sock on your hand, you can create a creature.
3) You are less self-conscious with the sock on your hand.

As the class period winds down, I ask each student to write a White Sock Monologue for our next meeting. You can handle this assignment in a variety of different ways. You can take some time out to discuss and define a monologue, giving them short examples to model. I usually use the points we made in the previous lessons about what makes a storytelling experience exciting and interesting. You could refer back to the stories about the fish and ask the students what they would do to these stories to transform them into monologues. Whatever you decide to do, the end result is that you are asking for a one-page monologue to be performed by the white sock puppet for the rest of the class.

The kids don't memorize their monologues. I give them some class time to practice and polish their performances. While they practice, I circulate around the theater giving praise and helpful hints on how to improve their monologues. It's quite a sight, seeing them all spread out in our theater space, rehearsing their monologues with plain white socks on their hands!

(NOTE: Some students will inevitably ask to attach eyes, nose, etc. to the white sock. This really defeats the purpose of expressing emotions with the use of only two elements: the white sock and the hand.)

Keeping assessment to a few simple points allows the students to concentrate on and improve a variety of skills. I usually use the following points:
1) Story line
2) Communication of emotion

3) Characterization
4) Enunciation
5) Projection

•   •   •

THE WHITE SOCK PUPPET PERFORMANCE (CLASS 7)

Set up a table with a cloth over it for the "stage." The cloth is important because it will "eat up" the sound, showing the young performer how vital it is to project and enunciate. After each student performs, we critique.

AN EXPLANATION OF HOW WE CRITIQUE

Before we critique a piece in class, I prepare the class in advance. I talk about positive comments and constructive criticism, giving an example of what is acceptable and what is not. What is at stake is the development of a student's confidence onstage for this particular project and for the rest of their performance life. This may sound a bit intense but many parents tell me stories about a bad experience in some dramatic production that destroyed their self-confidence. An offhand remark by a teacher or a student in a critique can damage the self-confidence or risk-taking abilities that students may have developed. After all, being critiqued in public is a frightening experience. I try to keep the comments short and to the point. Sometimes I have the class write them down, and then after I review them, give them to the young performers. It's a balancing act: A student in drama needs to learn how to accept criticism, but in educational theater a youngster also needs to develop a strong sense of self onstage that is a direct result of the critique. Using a critique to become a better performer is the goal.

The entire class period is devoted to these one- or two-minute monologues and their critiques. I am always surprised at the time and care the students take with some of their monologues and the unique characters that come to life with just a white sock on a student's hand. I summarize the lessons learned before class ends, using specific student examples.

• • •

READING OTHER PUPPET SCRIPTS (CLASSES 8, 9, AND 10)

The next few lessons concentrate on reading and analyzing scripts. If students are going to write a puppet show, it is helpful to read some existing scripts to gain insight into what they'd want to include in theirs. *Plays* magazine published by Plays, Inc. has good examples of puppet show scripts. For these readings, divide the students into groups. These groups can be the same groups as the B.O.P. project groupings, or they can be a random selection of students. There is a big plus to using the B.O.P. groups—they can start to learn to work together toward a goal. It is also interesting to see the group dynamics develop as they read aloud and analyze the scripts.

I usually give two or three short (one- or two-page) scripts to a group. The students are asked to assign parts and read the plays aloud. After they finish reading all of the puppet plays, they should compile lists of elements that the plays have in common, elements that make the puppet show interesting, and elements that they might want to include in their own puppet shows.

When all the groups have finished the read-throughs and have their lists, I make a master list on the board of puppet show elements. The students discover for themselves what works and what doesn't. They discover things like "dialogue works better than long sections of narration" or "elaborate settings do not work as well as interesting characters." As a class, we decide what key elements should be included in every script. We make up a list of requirements that looks something like this:

1) The story line should be very clear.
2) There should be a definite beginning, middle, and end.
3) The story should have a moral.
4) Conflict is essential and dialogue should be short and to the point.
5) Characters should be named carefully. These characters should be unique.
6) A resolution of the conflict at the end should be satisfying to the audience.
7) There should be four scenes.
8) The setting should be clearly indicated at the beginning of each scene.
9) Character descriptions should be listed at the beginning of the script as well as the time period in which the show takes place.
10) The shows should be five to seven minutes in length

We are now ready to begin the final project, Bag of Puppets.

• • •

B.O.P. (CLASSES 11–16)

At this point, the students have asked me at the beginning of every class, at least a dozen times, "When are we going to get the bag of puppets?" Before I give them the bags, I review, once again, puppet etiquette. I want the puppets to last a long time and they cannot survive if people are throwing them around. The consequences for a breach in puppet etiquette are severe because it is really important to teach respect for someone else's property.

I ask them to sit together as a group. (If you haven't announced the B.O.P. groups before this, then you can do that now.) I hand out a sheet of paper with the goals to accomplish for each class period. This form is reproduced at the end of the book. We review the form together. I explain to them that they are not only being graded on their performance, but on how they use class time.

For example—the first class goals are:

1) Name the characters.
2) Write a short but complete character description.
3) Decide on the moral or theme of the story.
4) Choose a setting for each scene.
5) Draft a rough outline of the action in each of the four scenes.

These requirements can be adapted to fit your particular schedule. Every year I change the requirement sheet, adding suggestions from students who have finished the project and fine-tuning it to match the particular student groupings.

They should assign a group secretary to keep records, notes, and copies of the script and all revisions. I give them a folder to keep everything together. At the end of each class, this secretary checks in with me. I mark a check, check minus, or a check plus in my grade book for their effort and organization. This check-in holds them responsible for the work and helps them use class time to the best advantage. Another important point is that the teacher should collect and keep the folders. If a student is absent, then the group can continue to work because the teacher has the folder.

FINALLY, I give the groups their puppets. I circulate around to make sure that there aren't any fights over who gets which puppet. At the end of the first B.O.P. class, I collect the puppets. The groups are not allowed to have them back until they have a completed script. It's a great way to get them to work hard, and it saves on the wear and tear of the puppets.

•　　•　　•

WRITING THE SCRIPT
(CLASSES 12, 13, AND 14)

The next classes are devoted to writing. The script that the students write must contain the elements discovered by the class in Lessons 8, 9, and 10. There are deadlines to be met with each class period. The groups should work independently around the classroom. This keeps them from overhearing what other groups are doing and copying their ideas. The surprise of watching another show for the first time and trying to figure out the theme is a lot of fun for the students. It also helps the performing group understand if they have been clear in their plotting and story line.

It usually takes two or three classes for the groups to come up with a completed script. Someone in the group is responsible for typing up the final draft. Every group member should have a copy as well as the teacher. Double, and even triple, spacing leaves room for revision.

I circulate from group to group during these classes. Striking a balance between telling them what to do and giving them options they can choose from is very important. I ask a lot of questions to keep everyone on track. This is one of the best times in the unit. The kids come up with the most amazing story lines and characters. The relationships between the unrelated puppets need to be imaginative. I tell them that their stories shouldn't bear resemblance to anything I've seen on TV or at the movies. They should be original. I also have a no-violence rule. The script can't have any physical violence between the puppets. They have to solve their conflicts with a creative approach.

The group's dynamics are really interesting to watch. Some students take the lead and begin to complete the goals. Some students are happy to sit back and let others do the work. When they are reminded that their classmates will be giving them a grade on their day-to-day contributions, they usually join in the planning with energy and focus.

•   •   •

REHEARSAL (CLASSES 15 AND 16)

When the scripts are ready, the groups get their puppets back so that they can practice. I usually allow two class periods for rehearsal. Again, the teacher should circulate during this process, side-coaching, asking questions to help the students polish their performances. I really try to avoid offering too much advice. This is *their* performance, not mine. Part of the learning comes from mistakes they've made that only become apparent in performance. If you are planning on doing this as a public performance—that is, a performance for an audience other than their classmates—you might want to give them more time to rehearse and polish their scripts.

If you have a performance area with a place for students to practice (behind a table or in an elaborate puppet theater) rotate the groups through, giving each group a chance to practice with the puppet stage. I watch these run-throughs and offer suggestions. This experience helps them realize the difficulty of juggling scripts and puppets, as well as the need to project and enunciate behind the walls of a puppet theater or from under a table.

•   •   •

FINAL PERFORMANCE (CLASS 17)

The final show can be handled in a variety of ways. Some years I videotape their shows. The video allows you to freeze their performance in time. With the ability to fast-forward and rewind, you can critique specific things in the performance, allowing students to see what they did and to learn from it.

Another choice is to have the students perform live for the entire class, making sure that the audience is jotting down their critiques as they watch. The assessment chart for B.O.P. is in the back of the book. The main problem with this approach is that the audience/evaluators may spend more time writing down comments than in watching the puppet shows.

Having a tape of the performance also allows you to share the shows with a different class section. I use the same bags of puppets for every class section, and they are fascinated to see how other classes use the same puppets in very different stories. Some years, the tape is taken home for the parents to see.

All of these choices depend on your class and your space, and they can be adapted to suit your needs.

•   •   •

WATCHING THE SHOWS

We have the best time watching the shows. The students take a random group of puppets and show strong relationships between them, in spite of their differences. Frogs get along with birds, a praying mantis shows the way home to a group that gets lost, and a cow bell signals the return of a very slow snail. The puppet shows reflect what is on the students' minds: their hopes, their fears, their future dreams. Many of the shows are about fitting in and being kind to one another. They present strong and valid ways to deal with all kinds of problems.

The best puppet shows can be performed for an assembly of the entire middle school. The teacher has to judge how public you want to make this assignment. If you are planning to widen the audience outside your classroom walls, it's only fair to let the students know how much exposure their show is going to have. Nothing hurts a student's developing self-confidence more than a last-minute decision to throw them out there in front of their peers or parents without any warning. Keeping students safe and confident onstage is vital to the development of their self-confidence. Working behind a puppet gives these youngsters a chance to take risks that they wouldn't normally take.

•   •   •

REFLECTION (CLASS 18)

The discussions that take place after the performances are modeled after the White Sock Puppet Monologues' critiques. For these discussions, the students use the critique form they filled out as they watched the shows. There is also a space on the form for them to evaluate their group work and their own work. These evaluations must be confidential. It is always surprising to me how honest the students are in these forms. When I combine my assessment with those of the students, a very clear picture comes into focus about the impact this unit has on their lives. There is a huge amount of work and learning that takes place. I have *never* had a year when I am not overwhelmed when I read these reflections. The students learn so much! How to work together to achieve a goal, compromising to move forward, how to refine a script—the list goes on and on. These forms are very important to me because the students are very clear about what worked and what didn't. I change the unit every year because of these suggestions. Telling the students how much I appreciate their suggestions lets them know we are all fellow-learners on this journey.

•   •   •

COMMUNITY CONNECTIONS

This project can be connected to a variety of other disciplines. Asking your students to write their scripts about themes centering on science, math, grammar, or social studies would involve some research that could connect with these other teachers. A puppet performance about recycling or ecological problems could be used in conjunction with a lesson being taught in science class. Puppet shows about the metric system could help students review for a test. We have even used all of my insect puppets to teach lessons on particular traits that certain kinds of insects have. In these shows, the insect used a natural ability to save the day.

If you connect with the art teacher, the puppets could even be made in class. The randomness of the combinations of unrelated puppets would happen when you create the student groups. Make sure you allow plenty of time for the puppets to be completed—papier-mâché takes a long time to dry.

Connections with social studies and English are a bit easier to see. Themes from a piece of literature could be used as the theme for an entire class of puppet shows. In social studies, students could write their puppet show about an historical character or event. They could do an *Animal Farm* interpretation of a particular event. Brainstorming the connections with other teachers will give you ideas that are exciting and imaginative.

You might decide to tour the shows. Before you venture outside the classroom walls, know the comfort level of your students. If your major focus is to keep your students safe onstage to develop self-confidence, you may want to make this unit a production that is shared only with the immediate class. If you have students whose self-confidence is high, you can make a variety of public performances available to a wider audience.

Elementary schools are a wonderful resource. Younger audiences are less threatening to middle school performers. It is a challenging audience, though. Preparation for your students is essential. Young children will talk to the puppets, run behind the scenes to see what is under or behind the puppet theater, or laugh and clap at the most awkward times. Your students should be prepared for almost anything. Your class may be able to lead a short discussion with the younger students, especially if the subject is about ecology or manners or such. One year my class did a joint puppet show with the younger students. My students did the voices and the younger ones manipulated the puppets. We needed lots of practice time, but it was worth it. For months afterward, the younger students would see the older ones on campus and yell out, "There's my puppet pal."

At the heart of all this, whether you use these performances to connect with your kids or to connect with the community at large, the puppets are a source of imagination stretching while staying safely behind the scenes. They will spark your students' creativity and help them gain confidence in performance. You will be surprised at the amount of learning that happens when an inanimate object is given the voice of your students.

• • •

TIME LINE FOR THE B.O.P. PROJECT

Introduction and Warm-ups: Classes 1–3
White Sock Puppet and Monologue: Classes 4–7
Researching the Script: Classes 8–10
B.O.P.: Classes 11–16
Performance: Class 17
Critique and Reflection: Class 18

CHAPTER TWO

Mask/Movement

GRADES SIX AND SEVEN

THE HISTORY BEHIND THE LESSON

I love masks almost as much as I love puppets. Their history is linked early on to drama, and I find the kinds of masks used throughout the ages fascinating. Masks worn by performers seem to take on a life of their own.

This lesson grew out of the desire to keep the sixth grade students safe onstage as they developed self-confidence. When a middle school student puts on a mask to act onstage, it gives the student something to hide behind, similar to the puppets in the B.O.P. project.

This chapter is designed to give students a chance to reflect on who they are and who they are becoming. Middle school is a time of discovery and confusion. These youngsters are not really children and not quite adults. At our school, the sixth graders are the youngest people in the Middle School. They want to fit in and be like everyone else and discover what makes them different than everyone else. I use the Mask/Movement unit to help them along their way.

BEFORE THE FIRST CLASS

For the first project in this unit you need to cut a mask template out of heavy cardboard. The template can be similar to the half-face masks of Halloween or they can be the vertical half of the face like the *Phantom of the Opera*. The half-face masks allow the students to see clearly. The students will use this template to trace the mask shape onto a sheet of lightweight cardboard and cut it out. After cutting out their masks, the students decorate their masks by creating a collage of images drawn or pasted on the mask. They then use it in a presentation along with a poem or prose piece about themselves.

You will also need to decide which materials you want to use to construct the second mask that will be used in the final performance. The first time I tackled this project, I talked to the art teacher about constructing the masks in her classroom. She was positive and supportive, and the masks were incredible—made from papier-mâché, some were spectacularly large in size which read very well onstage. One problem we had to solve was to make sure that students could see while wearing the masks, especially in regard to peripheral vision. Once this problem was addressed, the students not only looked great but also could perform with confidence.

The problem with visibility prompted me to find a way to fit the masks more closely to the young performers' faces. We have used plaster cast bandages to construct the masks in recent years. These masks are formed on the faces of the students making the fit almost perfect—visibility is not a problem—and the students can still personalize their masks with a variety of decorations to show character and emotion.

You can purchase the materials to make the plaster cast–bandage masks through an art supply catalogue. I received a donation from a parent who is a doctor and used the bandages for casts. You also need to purchase plastic basins for holding the water in which you soak the bandages. I bought a king-size jar of Vaseline for slathering on their faces and it lasted for years.

Other supplies you need for the mask making include elastic, glue guns and glue sticks, paint brushes and paints.

Setting up stations where the students can work is a fantastic way to bring order out of chaos, but I will go into this later in the chapter. You can also enlist the aid of the art teacher in the decorating and painting of these plaster cast–bandage masks.

The music that you use for the movement part of the unit should be instrumental. Using something that the students are not familiar with challenges their imaginations. Music that inspires a story in your mind as you listen to it is the one to choose. I was lucky enough to have a partner in developing this unit who knew a lot about experimental and electronic music. The pieces that we eventually chose were a real challenge to our students and forced them to come up with imaginative scenarios for our final performances. Your students will use the emotions they feel as they listen to the music as inspiration for their masks. It is important for the music to have strong story-line possibilities and a variety of emotional variations. Classical music can also inspire students. A music teacher can be a marvelous resource.

• • •

THE FIRST CLASS

I begin with a short overview of the unit. A sheet of paper with due dates and an explanation of the main project work help students understand what is going to happen during this unit. Let your students know that the schedule is subject to change. I have found that day-to-day middle school life intrudes on the best-laid plans and the minute I pass out any kind of schedule, I have to modify it because of a field trip or assembly!

A discussion about masks in general leads to the making of a long list of masks that are used today. We talk about professions that use masks and the reason that they are so important. Sometimes I bring in examples from my own mask collection and pass them around for the students to examine. I show two excellent videos about the history of the mask-making tradition from a company called Film for the Humanities, Inc. Students are asked to take notes on the video and give a short quiz on the material. I also ask them to jot down ideas of material they might use to decorate their masks as they watch the video. After the quiz we discuss the ideas in the video and gain a sense of the history of masks in different cultures. If you can persuade an art teacher to come in to lecture on mask making or take a virtual trip to an art museum to look at ancient masks, it can give students a deeper understanding of the long and rich tradition they are about to experience.

The next discussion we have in class is about invisible masks that we wear every day. They read some poetry I have collected on the masks people wear. One that works especially well can be found in a book by Carol Painter *Friends Helping Friends,* published by Educational Media Corporation. This poem speaks of

the ever concealing mask.
Beneath dwells the real me,
in confusion and fear, in loneliness…
Who am I, you may wonder?

We talk about how difficult it is to drop our masks and let the person we really are shine through. Sometimes we even get into the times when it is necessary to wear a mask. I give them a sheet entitled, "Notes on Myself" with some questions for them to answer. (See page 121 for this sheet.) With some classes I have circled just a few of the questions for them to answer, with other classes I have asked them to answer all of the questions. You know your students and can make that judgment call. I tell them that I am looking for serious, honest answers and let them know that these answers will be used to help them with our next project.

When they finish answering the questions, they pair up and

share their responses with their partner. We re-group as a class after ten to fifteen minutes and talk about getting to know the "real" person behind the mask. I ask them if they could introduce their partners to the rest of the class now that they know more about them. They usually ask if that's what we are going to do next and I tell them yes—but with a twist.

I pass out the lightweight cardboard and ask them to trace the mask template onto the cardboard and then cut it out. You can also cut out the masks in advance and just pass them out at this point. Then I assign some homework. "Take the masks home and do a collage of images that represent the answers on the questionnaire." For example, if the answer to the question "What is my greatest fear?" is spiders, then the student could put a picture of a spider on the mask. If the answer to the question "What is my favorite possession?" is my card collection then the student could paste a card onto the mask. I tell them that for the next class their partners will introduce them to the class. The person being introduced will simply stand there holding the mask in front of his or her face while the partner introduces them to the class. I ask them to use appropriate images on their masks and tell them that they will receive a grade on the craftsmanship of the mask and the introduction. They will have class time to practice the introductions before they get up to present their partners.

●　　●　　●

THE MASK OF SELF AND POEM (CLASSES 2 AND 3)

The next class, I give them about fifteen minutes to meet with their partners and work out an introduction. Then they deliver the intro to the class. I usually assess these presentations with point values and use it as a quiz grade.

I have also tried a variation on this exercise, asking students to fill out a questionnaire but not pairing them up. We discuss some of the answers to the questions as a class, and I ask for at might symbolize those answers. Then the homework mask collage is assigned, but with one twist. I ask them a look at their finished mask and write a short poem that could be titled, "The Me of Me." The culmination of this project is the delivery of the poem while holding their mask in front of their face. I give them 10 points for the project—assessing the craftsmanship of the mask and the delivery of the poem.

After all the students have performed, we discuss what it felt like to be "behind the mask." This discussion is very informative and important because you will be able to discern any fears that your students have about performing behind a mask. The discussion may raise questions as to how the students are going to show emotion without the use of their faces. The teacher should listen carefully to what the students say and address their questions with answers that will give them confidence onstage.

After this discussion, we are ready to listen to some music.

• • •

THE MOVEMENT (CLASS 4)

The next class begins with a quiet listening session. I ask them to listen to a piece of music with their eyes closed. We discuss the kinds of emotions we felt as we listened to the music. I ask how they would show those emotions onstage—just through movement. I replay the music and ask for volunteers to move to the music showing their emotion. Sometimes I will volunteer first, which creates a lot of laughter and breaks the tension.

Sometimes we play an improvisational game called Walk the Talk. The class lines up onstage facing me. I make sure that they spread out and have a good amount of space between them. This game can get a bit rowdy. Then I explain the game. I will start at the beginning of the line and ask the student to think of an emotion. Then they move forward to the front of the stage (or, if you don't have a stage, they can move forward about ten feet) showing the emotion in the way they move. Then they turn around, face the group, and say the word describing the emotion. When they say the word, they say it in a particular style, using their voices to give color and drama to the word. Then the rest of the class, who have been watching and listening very carefully, moves toward the front of the stage, imitating as exactly as possible, the movement of this student. Then they turn around and mimic the voice intonation of the word. I usually do the first word because it breaks the ice. I will walk in a slow and lazy manner and then turn slowly toward the class and say "ennui." Then they imitate my movement and intonation. This exercise gives even the shy kids a chance to risk onstage with emotion, movement, and intonation.

Then I ask them to write their name and an emotion on a sheet of paper and give it to me. I ask them to walk around the stage showing the emotion. I usually show them what I want by being the first to do the exercise, just to break the ice. The class, acting as the audience, has to guess the emotion that the performer is trying to communicate. After they finish, I praise them for their efforts and offer helpful hints as to how they can improve their performances. After everyone has taken a turn, we discuss how to make emotions stronger in our performance by using our bodies. This discussion ends the fourth class. Now, we are ready to listen to the songs for the final Mask/Movement presentation.

• • •

THE MUSIC (CLASS 5)

The class is split into groups. I usually have two groups per class. Each group gets one song and listens quietly to the first play-through. Then they are to discuss and brainstorm possible themes, ideas, and story lines. They listen to the song again and begin to come up with one theme they agree on. They should also discuss emotions that they feel as they listen to the song and chose an emotion to play in the story. The emotion that they chose drives the character and mask making.

For example—one student says she feels sadness upon listening to the music. She wants to play a character whose main emotion is sadness. Her mask will be constructed to show sadness—and it is the responsibility of the group to write a character that is sad into the story line. Another student feels anger, another silliness. The story line includes anger, silliness, and sadness. Everyone takes part in the wordless drama. The music is played over and over again while the story is created, refined, practiced, and revised. A final draft is written with plenty of space for changes and corrections, with a copy for every student and the teacher. This takes one class period.

If the students are making the masks in art class, then they should begin with rough sketches of how their masks will look. If you are making the plaster cast–bandage masks in class—now is the time to begin.

•   •   •

MAKING THE PLASTER CAST MASKS
(CLASSES 6–8)

The first time I made these masks with the sixth grade, I enlisted the help of my older students. I had the sixth graders pair up, and each pair had an eleventh or twelfth grade student as a helper/supervisor. In subsequent years, I did the project with less help and a lot of organization and preparation. It worked out very well, with a minimum of chaos.

The materials needed for this project follow:

- 16 strips 1"x8" of plaster cast–bandage material for a half-face mask (available through art or medical supply stores)
- Sandpaper

- 1 large jar of petroleum jelly to seal the skin and provide for easy mask removal
- 1 small 10' x 5' plastic container for water
- Newspapers or drop cloths to cover any working areas

Students should bring in an old shirt to wear while mask making to protect their clothes. They should also bring in a washcloth, towel, and whatever they use to cleanse their faces.

We make *half*-face masks for a number of reasons. One reason is that the students can project their voices a lot easier with a half-face mask. Students who are claustrophobic don't have to have straws stuck up their nose to breathe while getting their masks made. These half-face masks give the students a chance to use part of their face for expression. The half-face masks still provide a new identity but are much more flexible for characterization. It also is cost-effective to use less of the material to make the masks.

I have the students work in pairs. We have long tables set up to work on. One student is on the table getting a mask done on their face by their partner. It takes about forty minutes to do one student mask. This includes setup and cleanup.

One student slathers his face with Vaseline—especially the eyebrows and hairline. The partner puts about one foot of warm water in the basin. The student who is having the mask made on his face lies down on the table and his partner begins—one bandage at a time—to dip the strips into the warm water, to let the strip drip dry a bit, and to then layer these strips on her partner's face. The strips should not be placed into the hairline as the removal of the dried mask can be painful. Folding the strips back onto themselves, instead of into the hairline, works well.

I usually play some soothing music to keep everyone calm and relaxed. The student who is having the mask layered on his face needs to remain perfectly still so the mask sets up and follows the contours of the face for a good fit.

When all the bandage strips are used up in the layering, the student should remain still for seven to ten minutes and the teacher should check the mask for strength. The temple area where the elastic will be attached should be especially reinforced. The mask warms up as it dries and gets very hard. If the students have used too much water in the dipping process, then the mask takes longer to dry.

When the mask is solid and relatively dry, the student sits up and removes it from his face. He should begin to work his fingers around at the hairline with his face toward the ground. Gravity helps with the removal. The mask comes off slowly and hurts a bit, like a bandage when you are removing it.

The masks need a place—a shelf or a bookcase—to continue to air dry completely. It should be a place where the masks are safe from youngsters picking them up to look at them. Too much handling during this phase can spoil the integrity of a mask.

• • •

DECORATING THE MASKS
(CLASSES 9 AND 10)

Set up stations for the mask decorating. I have a painting station with brushes, tempera, and water; a station set up with a couple of hot glue guns, and a station with water and extra bandages for students to reinforce their masks. If you can find someone to help you supervise, it is a big help.

Some students bring in materials to decorate their masks. One thing I do before they get into decorating their masks is to ask them for a simple sketch of how they visualize the mask. I like to see the emotion they have chosen to play and to offer suggestions for decorating that will read onstage. The students need to think BIG. Enlarged features like eyebrows, cheekbones, and noses can be accented by simply adding more bandage strips.

The masks must be completely dry to paint. I also punch holes in the temples of the masks for the elastic. Make sure that when the students are decorating their masks, they don't plug up the holes!

Some students try to attach heavy materials to their masks. Always have them try on the mask to see if these materials are going to work. Sometime you can see in advance that these materials will be too heavy to wear or attach to the half-face masks. Some students may want to trim and sand the rough parts of their mask to make it more comfortable to wear.

It takes us two class periods for decorating and painting the masks. I allow a week of mask drying before we begin decorating. During the waiting period, I have the students work on writing their story line and rehearsing.

•   •   •

THE STORY LINE AND REHEARSAL PERIOD (CLASSES 11, 12, AND 13)

Each group has a CD player and starts by listening to the music. Then the story line is constructed. Every student must be written into the play. These plots use the emotions around which their masks have been designed. The plots range from the simple narratives to the absurd. Some years the students have simply entered the stage/space and moved in time to the music in a celebration of a variety of emotions onstage. Some years they have written very complex stories. Whatever your students decide to do, the masks and the music are the inspiration for the scripts. Everything must be written down, using the format of a play. Sometimes I require a set number of scenes. It all depends on the group.

The groups work independently on writing their scripts. The groups check in with me at the beginning of class and we decide on the goal for that particular class. We set goals for each class period. This keeps them writing and focused. They also know that I will be assessing them on the completion of these goals. A goal might be the completion of a rough draft, three solid rehearsals, or a rewrite of the script. I circulate around during class listening and offering suggestions. At the end of class, I take about five minutes to check in with them and see if they have accomplished what they set out to do.

SOME EXAMPLES OF STORY LINES

One year we had an entire story line centered around kids who were trick or treating. They were set upon by bullies who stole their candy. Then they were rescued by a character named Super Josh. The mask of this character was HUGE—a large redhead with freckles and ears that stuck out. The entire story was inspired by the music and had a beginning, a middle, and an end, but not one word was spoken. Large body pantomime was used to convey the story.

One year, I worked with a group of girls and my collaborator, Matt, worked with a group of boys. The girls' performance was a celebration of a series of emotions. Each character made an entrance to the music and moved across the stage showing her emotion in a variety of ways. At the end of the piece, all the characters came onstage doing a short dance and then posed and froze for the ending.

The boys group, working with Matt, did a movement piece that used a stylized slow-motion battle. One student was the instigator of the conflict between the two warring groups. This character eventually wins the battle—but he is the only one left after the battle—so the question was posed by the group—"Who wins when there is conflict and war?" We had some spirited discussions after the performance as we tried to answer the question they had posed.

You may prefer to take an existing story line and have the students make masks for their characters in the story. I have worked with older students (ninth and tenth grade) on the tales of Beowulf, Medusa, Childe Roland, and "The Giant's Steps" (a Celtic tale). These tales gave the students a chance to make some startling and elaborate character masks. We toured the shows within our school community—presenting the tales to the fifth, sixth, and seventh grades.

• • •

THE FINAL PERFORMANCES (CLASS 14)

We invited the seventh and eighth grade students to an in-school performance of the Mask/Movement Project. I had two classes: Each performed two dramas, giving us four pieces to perform. It took about thirty-five minutes for the entire performance. I told my sixth graders at the beginning of the project that we would be presenting for the rest of the Middle School. If you are going to present this exciting project for parents, elementary children, or the general public, your middle school students need to be aware of that from the beginning. They can prepare themselves mentally for the stress of a performance in front of their peers, their parents, or the public. Some years I've decided that their self-confidence would suffer if we performed for their peers. During those years we performed for the other sixth grade, or I invited a couple of elementary school classes to the performances. Choosing an audience carefully has its advantages when it comes to developing a sixth grade performer's self-confidence.

• • •

ASSESSMENT AND REFLECTION (CLASS 15)

I have mentioned a few ways to assess a variety of stages during the process of this unit: short quizzes, goals' achievement during class, and craftsmanship during mask construction. This is such an active unit that I include things like classroom clean-up, having materials ready for use, and proper use of those materials as points of assessment. I also make sure that the students know from the beginning of the unit that they are being graded on these points. It sometimes helps to motivate constructive behavior throughout the project.

After the final performance, I ask the students to answer a short questionnaire to give me their honest opinions of the project. I have used these student suggestions to improve and change the project each year.

For the final performance assessment, I give points for large body movement; integration of music, story, and movement; and the effective portrayal of emotions. As a teacher of drama, you can choose to emphasize whatever part of the unit you wish.

• • •

COMMUNITY CONNECTIONS

Having an artist or an art teacher work alongside you is the best of all possible situations. Making connections with a music teacher who is teaching a unit on electronic music can be very exciting. Language arts and social studies can provide your classes with mythologies and legends to perform. Choosing stories from Asia, Africa, Russia, or any other country and performing these tales with masks involves the students in a way that they will remember for a long time. A certain theme from a language arts class could drive your choice of music, story line and mask making. For example, our language arts teacher does a unit on the hero in literature. You could require the stories to have some heroic deed at the center of its action. The students can perform and then discuss the theme afterward.

One year, we used music that was composed of insect sounds. You could connect with your science teacher and present a performance with bug masks—perhaps even using the way that an insect moves as an inspiration for the movement part of the project.

Don't let the possible messiness or complexity of this unit discourage you from trying it with your students. It is one of the most popular activities at our school, and the most memorable dramatic activity of my alumni students. Getting some enthusiastic collaborators to help you out spreads the excitement around. It is worth the risk, which happens to be exactly the same lesson that you are trying to teach your students in drama!

• • •

TIME LINE FOR MASK/MOVEMENT

Introductory Lesson: Class 1
The Mask of Self and Poem: Classes 2 and 3
The Movement and Music: Classes 4 and 5
Plaster Cast–Mask Construction: Classes 6–8
Decorating the Masks: Classes 9 and 10
Story line and Rehearsal: Classes 11–13
Final Performance: Class 14
Reflection: Class 15

CHAPTER THREE

Clan Drama: Solving a Mystery

GRADES SEVEN AND EIGHT

THE HISTORY BEHIND THE LESSON

We know that the first theater took place thousands of years ago around campfires, where the people of ancient cultures gathered, telling stories, trying to make sense of the mysterious universe in which they lived. I wanted to introduce a unit to my middle school students that illustrated how that early form of drama began.

Middle school students are constantly trying to make sense of changes in their universe. I decided that perhaps the dramas that they encountered every day were not all that different from those of our ancestors.

I came up with a project called the Clan Drama. I used it with my seventh grade students during the first quarter, meeting twice a week for forty minutes. Over the years, I've also used it with grade eight and modified it several times, and if you try it, you'll probably want to refine it further to suit your own school environment.

The main emphasis has remained the same: the creation of a story by an ancient group that explains some fundamental mystery of the universe. The thrust of the unit is to teach students that, essentially, drama is rooted in our souls. Creating stories is how we make sense of our world and the human experience.

• • •

BEFORE THE FIRST CLASS

Before your first class, create groups of four to six students. These are the Clans. I usually create three or four kinds of clans, each assigned a different geographic habitat, i.e., *Desert Clan, Forest Clan, Plains Clan,* and *Arctic Clan.* If you know the students well, try to put a couple of self-starters with kids who need direction. It will help group dynamics and improve the students' ability to work together.

Next, make up a set of mystery index cards—one card for each group and a couple of extra to give them choices. Each card should include their habitat, (desert, forest, etc.) and one question. Here's a list of the mystery cards I've used with my students, including extra questions if you need them.

1) **Desert Clan.** How was water given to the clan? How did the scorpion get its sting? How did the cactus get its spines?

2) **Forest Clan.** How did the Earth begin? Why are there earthquakes? How did lightning come to be?

3) **Plains Clan.** Why is there drought and then rain? How did the clan receive the gift of corn and peppers (or some other vegetable)? How did bread come to be?

4) **Arctic Clan.** How did the whale come to be? What are the northern lights? Where does the snow come from?

There are many other mysteries of nature that puzzled the ancient mind and are connected with a particular habitat. After you do the project once, you'll probably come up with some mystery questions of your own. For example, the answers to "How did the Earth come to be?" would vary because the clans' distinctive environments would be reflected in the elements of the story. When I first introduce the lesson, I try to put as much emphasis as possible on the fact that the students are part of an ancient clan. It forces them to really use their imaginations to go back in time, when nature seemed dangerous and wonderful but was not explainable in modern scientific terms.

•   •   •

THE FIRST CLASS

You can have some real fun introducing this project. I'm a bit of a ham, so I dim the lights and wear something appropriate, like a long, wildly printed dress and a fur vest, and say,

"I am the Great Shaman. I have gathered you here today for a feast, a time when all the clans come together to share the mysteries of life. We will create stories to share with each other to help explain the beautiful and dangerous land around us."

Then I get them into their groups and tell them that the first thing they must do is assign someone to keep the records of the clan. It should be someone responsible, with good writing skills. This person, known as the Mighty Records-Keeper, will keep a journal of all the work that the clan does on their project. This journal log is very important—it becomes, in essence, a clan's script. To help insure that it all stays together, I give each clan a manila folder to keep their records together and suggest that the Clan members decorate the folders with the sign of their clan, a sort of family coat of arms.

If your middle school students are anything like mine, you know the kinds of things that can happen if a student is allowed to keep the group's work in a locker. So I usually collect the journals at the end of each class because the Mighty Records-Keeper might get the flu (or lose the journal) and then the clan wouldn't be able to do its work.

After I introduce the students to the project and divide them into their clans, I let each group choose a mystery card. I tell them that their clan is to create a drama that clearly explains the mystery to the other clans. Every group member must have a part in the drama. Again, I emphasize that they must remember that they are members of an ancient culture and that their drama must reflect this. The point is, no clan drama should resemble a TV sit-com or action movie. I urge my students to use their own creativity and imagination to create their own story.

Each clan receives a handout (see pages 125–126) with the requirements for their performance—the culmination of their work. Included in the handout are the goals of each class period and the goals for the entire project. I give a grade for the completion of each of the goals. I tell them that the Great Shaman will be checking on the completion of these goals and that part of their grade will be based on meeting the deadlines. To keep them on task, I include a five-minute check-in time before class ends in which I talk to each Mighty Records-Keeper about the progress of their clan's story.

● ● ●

CREATING THE MYTHS (CLASSES 2 AND 3)

For the next two classes, the clans fashion their own mythology. They create a name for their clan and for each member. They design a clan symbol, which they can use to decorate their manila folder. They also write a history explaining who they are, where they live, and what they believe in. It can be very simple, or really detailed if the group takes hold of the idea. The history should be at least two typed pages in length.

Each group needs to discuss their mystery and come up with a script outline, including plot summary, character, setting, and scene and character descriptions. The drama must be five to ten minutes in running time and include at least three distinct scenes. I also asked that they find a way to include a representation of their clan symbol, just to strengthen the identity of each group.

AN EXAMPLE OF A MYTH

The Forest Clan name themselves the MaJoJuNis (a clever combination of everyone's first two initials). Their symbol is the pine tree with an owl perched in it. They have created a clan history that explains why they live in the forest, how they construct their homes, what their diet consists of, and the hierarchy of their clan. Their mystery card wants an explanation of the origins of their universe, a creation myth. With lots of discussion, arguments, and collaboration, they agree on the outline as follows:

> PLOT SUMMARY: The world began with a lone pine tree in the deep darkness. The Great Green God saw that the pine was a strong and tall tree, perfect for perching. The GGG created an owl to perch in the tree. The owl was a magical creature who, when she spread her wings and flew during the darkness, created the oceans and the mountains and the forests. She flew again and all the animals were created. After this flight, the owl cried "WHO" and man was created. Man had to learn how to respect the trees, animals, and so on. The owl was his guide.

> SCENES: Scene 1 The Darkness
> Setting: Nothing onstage
>
> Scene 2 The First Day of Flight
> Setting: Oceans, rivers, mountains

Scene 3 The Second Day of Flight
Setting: The forest

Scene 4 The Loneliness and Calling Forth of Man
Setting: A forest

Scene 5 The Teaching of Man
Setting: A forest

CHARACTERS:

The Voice of the Great Green God: A kind and benevolent
   being who speaks with dignity
The Pine Tree: A majestic yet humble tree that wants to help
   shelter the birds and animals
The Owl: A silent, dignified spirit with a love for all creation
Man: Reckless, naïve, yet eager to learn
Assorted animals and birds

The students must give specific character traits. This invites them to enter into characterization. Often they rush right into the creation of dialogue, forgetting that they need to give time and thought to the structure of the drama. The more time and care that they take in these structuring exercises, the deeper and clearer their drama will be. It is helpful to remind them of this.

•   •   •

COSTUMES AND PROPS (CLASS 4)

I let the kids pick their costumes and props after they've created their mythology, but before they write their script. An outlandish costume or clever prop might spark their imagination during the script-writing part of the process. I've collected a big trunk of costumes that consist of old fur, fake fur pieces, robes, fake vines and flowers, crowns made of leaves, feathers, and various other bits of clothing. Each year I add to the collection.

The kids can also find costumes at home or make them at school. One year, a Forest Clan made giant leaves out of large pieces of cardboard, attached them at the top with string and wore them over their clothing. Even the suggestion of a costume (like a hat or a swatch of fur tied at the waist) helps them get into character. Some old curtains draped over risers creates an atmosphere of a cave and we add a great fake campfire that my students love to use. The fact that it plugs in and turns on and off doesn't seem to matter to them!

For the most part, the students amaze me with the languages, dances, and mythologies they create. But inevitably, some clans will want to incorporate fight scenes into their stories, and that means weapons like spears or swords. While these kinds of props add a lot to the presentations, I tell my class at the outset that they must use invisible weapons. I also remind them that they should try to stretch their creativity and work to solve their problems without violence. When they do incorporate weapons into their stories, it becomes a challenge for them to learn how to mime their use so that it is clear to the audience what they are doing. With some classes, depending on the maturity of the group, I let them make blunted spears or cardboard tubes fashioned into swords. When they choreograph fight scenes, I am always there and I tell them that the scenes MUST be done in slow motion so no one gets hurt.

Some clans want to add music to their dramas. I have certain rules that I ask them to follow when choosing music. It must be instrumental. It should create a mood that transports the audience to an ancient time and place. Providing a variety of CDs for the students to listen to helps them understand what to look for in music. If they decide to use their own music, I reserve the right of censorship if it doesn't meet my standards.

•   •   •

WRITING THE SCRIPTS (CLASSES 5, 6, AND 7)

For the next several classes, each clan develops their scenes, adding action, conflict, and dialogue. I always remind my students not to rush immediately into dialogue, that it's important to develop their characters first, and to plan how their drama is going to be structured.

While everyone is working, I make my way from group to group, sitting in, silently at first, to observe group dynamics and offering help as needed. It's not easy to resist the urge to interfere with what your students are doing, but remind yourself that this is their creation and ownership is very important. When I do feel a need to intervene, I try to pose questions and get them to solve problems. For example, I might ask, "Do you think an audience will understand that part? How can you change it to make it clear?" Keep making the rounds, offering suggestions and praising their efforts. Traces of modern life will keep creeping into the clan's stories. Remind them again that they are an ancient culture and that their mythologies must reflect this.

You'll discover that some clans will come up with ideas that you've never thought about. Some might want to add a dance, or a chant, for instance. In one case, one of my student clans devised a new language and had a narrator translate during the presentation. It was very funny.

As each scene is created and copied by the Great Records-Keeper (who, by the way, I give extra credit or a break in the grading for all the extra work), he or she assigns the typing of the script to other students in the clan. By the end of the script-writing classes, the group ought to have a clearly readable mythology, triple-spaced for the changes that are inevitably going to happen once they start rehearsing. I never let a group begin rehearsing until they have completely finished their script.

Many times the kids will want to improvise the whole script. Improvisation is, of course, fine. In the case of the Clan Drama, I let them improvise only *after* they have a finished script. Here's why. While some of the best ideas happen when the kids improvise, I've found that if they rely on total improvisation they lose their way, forgetting the through-line of the play completely. The mythology tends to be a muddled mess. But if they improvise *after* they have a script, the improvisation adds a lot to an already existing story line.

• • •

REHEARSAL AND PERFORMANCE (CLASSES 8–12)

How much time you give to rehearsal depends on your students. I devote five classes to it: two for run-through and script changes; one for memorization; one with costumes, props, and music; and a final dress rehearsal.

I usually have the clan present their final performance for each other in class. We critique the dramas on a wide variety of points, but of greatest importance is how well the mystery question has been explained. After all the dramas have been presented, each clan performs them again without an audience so that I can videotape their work. Then I use the tape as an opportunity to critique the finer points of performing.

• • •

ASSESSMENT

I use three things to assess the project: my own evaluation based on meeting deadlines, group work, and the finished production; a detailed student self-assessment; and a confidential assessment in which the students evaluate the work of other members of their clan. All the forms can be found in the appendix.

I tell the class at the beginning of the project that they will be evaluating each other and themselves. Judging one another's work improves cooperation within the groups. In their confidential assessments, students are very honest about who did the work and who cooperated. My students are usually harder on themselves in their self-evaluations than I am. Employing all three of these assessment tools gives me a clear picture of the actual clan group dynamics from several different perspectives.

•   •   •

WRAP-UP AND REFLECTION (CLASSES 13 AND 14)

One of the best parts of the unit is reflection time. Watching the videotaped presentations, the students and I review what worked and what didn't. Everything from simple stage awareness, to vocal projection and through-line of the story become a lot more apparent as we sit together and watch the unedited video. I always make a point to find the strengths of each clan's production and bring them to the attention of the entire class. After the initial reflection period, we vote for the best production and talk about why we liked it. A student assignment sheet to use while viewing the videos is in the appendix.

One of the best things that the Clan Drama Unit does is open up a wide-ranging discussion of theater in general. I ask the students why they think we did this project and talk about the beginnings of the art of drama. We talk about humor in a play, and how it can add or detract. Some students use inside jokes in their dramas and we trade opinions about how everyone might not understand their use. I explain how costumes, music, and lights can enhance a production. We consider what makes an exciting play. We talk about the importance of working as a group and the need to compromise to achieve a goal.

Better than any other introductory lesson I've used, the Clan Drama piques the interest and understanding of students who are just discovering the art. In the creation of their own clans, they shape their own mythologies and therefore their own dramas. In turn, they discover that, through drama, they can make sense of their world and of the human experience. To me, that is what educational theater ought to do.

•   •   •

COMMUNITY CONNECTIONS

You do not have to limit the performance to the class—the dramas are particularly pertinent for social studies or anthropology classes. Elementary schools will enjoy the performances as well. But make sure that you tell your students from the very beginning that you plan to take their Clan Dramas on the road.

The Clan Drama could also be used, with some modifications, to illustrate how man explained the mysteries in other disciplines. Themes could drive the mystery cards that are given out. These themes could relate to math (How did the numerical system come into being?) and science (How did the oceans become salt water?) or art (Why do cave paintings exist?) and music (What is a song and who sang the first one?) Language arts classes might enjoy seeing certain themes come alive, themes like the hero in literature or how the alphabet was created. Even physical education class might want to introduce a unit on tennis or volleyball with a humorous look at how these sports began.

•   •   •

TIME LINE FOR THE CLAN DRAMA

Introduction/Setting up the Clans and the Mythology: Class 1
Creating the Myths: Classes 2 and 3
Securing Costumes and Props: Class 4
Writing the Scripts: Classes 5–7
Rehearsal and Performance: Classes 8–12
Watching the Videotape and Evaluating the Clan Dramas:
    Classes 13–14

CHAPTER FOUR

Giant Puppet Show
GRADES SEVEN AND EIGHT

THE HISTORY BEHIND THE LESSON

The first conference for theater teachers that I ever attended was held in Minneapolis. I took part in a puppetry workshop presented by the Heart of the Beast Puppet and Mask theater. We made our own puppets and presented an improvisational theatrical piece built around the creations. It was the first time I had performed in front of a large audience in a long time. But they were theater teachers, so they were a forgiving audience. Our performance made quite an impression, though. I am still meeting theater teachers years later that say, "Were you one of the puppet people in Minneapolis?" The puppets that we made were not the smallish kind. They were eight feet tall! It was so much fun manipulating these giant puppets that I was committed to finding a way to do this with my middle school students.

The project that grew from that experience is one of the most popular and successful things I have ever done with middle school. In fact, the idea for "Community Building Days," the last chapter of this book, came from the giant puppet shows. The possibilities of creating a wide variety of characters that are essentially inanimate objects until a performer brings them to life are endless. Making these characters larger than life is challenging but BIG puppets make BIG excitement.

Do not be daunted by the largeness of the project. The puppets we made were easy to put together. You can make them as simple or as complex as you like. We have made abstract puppets that challenged the creativity and imagination of the students, and we've made puppets for existing stories. Normally shy and retiring middle school students come alive onstage as they manipulate the giant puppets they have created. This project boosts storytelling ability, large and small movement, and self-confidence in a BIG way.

I must tell you that I did get help with this project right from the start, which made it so much easier. I enlisted the aid of a former drama student named Matt. Matt was in college studying studio art and wanted to become a teacher. Over his winter break, he helped design and construct the puppets with me. We co-taught the lesson to the seventh grade because he had another week of vacation. (I have also had success teaching this unit to eighth grade.) We ran rehearsals right up until he had to go back to college. If you can enlist the aid of an art teacher for this project, it helps to have another set of hands to guide the students. It also helps to have some help with the designing and preliminary sketches of the giant puppets.

•　　•　　•

BEFORE THE FIRST CLASS

We designed four ten-foot high puppets and about two dozen cardboard puppets that measured about three feet by four feet. Each class was divided into two groups and each group had one giant puppet (manipulated by three students) and about six smaller ones (one to each student). The materials you need are as follows:
- Twelve ten foot 2 x 2s
- Large pieces of cardboard

- A staple gun and staples
- Primer paint and tempera paint

The tools and miscellaneous items we used during the construction included:
- Paint brushes
- Drop cloths
- Matte knives
- Hot glue guns and hot glue sticks
- Duct tape

We wrapped the duct tape around the places where the students would be holding the wooden 2 x 2s to prevent splinters.

The giant puppet was made from three 10-foot 2 x 2s, large pieces of cardboard cut with matte knives, and some remnants of material. Matt and I went into school over winter break to cut the shapes and staple them onto the wood. The puppets were split into four distinct parts—a head, a body, and two hands. The head and body were stapled onto one of the 2 x 2s; a hand was stapled onto each of the two remaining 2 x 2s. The hands were connected to the body with material. (See illustration pages 56–57.) We did not decorate any of the cardboard pieces, leaving that for the students.

The smaller puppets were cut out of the smaller pieces of cardboard. The students would hold the sides of the cardboard shapes. If you wanted to, you could put handles on the backside of these smaller puppets. Some years we used both sides of the small puppets, so it was impossible to use a handle on the back. At a certain point in the story, the students flipped the puppets over and a different character would be on the reverse side.

• • •

THE FIRST CLASS WITH AN EXISTING STORY

The first class depends on the approach you take—whether you create your own story or whether you use a book or a story that already exists.

If you use an existing story, the first class should be a reading of the story out loud. A discussion of the types of characters that can be made into puppets follows, or if you have made that decision already, a look at the puppets you have cut out of the cardboard is next. The students need to decide who is going to manipulate the giant puppet (three students from each group) and who is going to use the small cardboard puppets.

•   •   •

CREATING THE PUPPETS (CLASSES 2–6)

We set up three or four stations for designing and decorating the puppets. Two stations had paint, another had hot glue guns, another had an adult cutting things with a matte knife. For one of the stories, we planned to have a reversible puppet; a "good" character on one side and a "nasty" character on the other. The smaller puppets also had a good character on one side and a bad character on the other. The students who manipulated the giant puppet were in charge of decorating it. They sketched and painted the cardboard and then we stapled it onto the wooden 2 x 2s. The other students designed their characters and we cut them out of the cardboard with the matte knives. They painted and decorated their puppets at another station. This process took four class periods, forty minutes each. We had a classroom where we could leave the stations up and just clean up the paints and such. This saved a LOT of time in setting up and tearing down.

•   •   •

BLOCKING AND REHEARSAL (CLASSES 7–11)

After the puppets are designed, constructed, and decorated, the blocking and rehearsal begins. With the reversible puppets, we needed to coordinate when we flipped the puppets and when the entrances and exits happened. We had one student who wanted to be the narrator, and another one wanted to run the tape player for the music that we put at the beginning and the end of the show. Rehearsals took about four or five class periods. We worked a lot on getting the giant puppet moving smoothly and showing characterization. The smaller cardboard puppets were easier to manipulate, but there were more of them. Finally the show began to fall into place and run as a polished piece.

• • •

PERFORMANCES (CLASS 12)

We performed these shows for our Lower School, grades K through 5. The giant puppets were showstoppers! When they made their entrances, the children gasped and then laughed and clapped. We also performed for a parent meeting, and it was proof positive that no matter what your age might be—everyone loves puppets.

• • •

ASSESSMENT

There are many skills developed with this unit. I place an emphasis on two main areas: process and product. The *process* was assessed on a day-to-day basis with check marks in such areas as puppet construction and cleanup. The rehearsal process was also assessed in such areas as focus and concentration, puppet manipulation, and creative approach to character creation. The *product* was the performance and the final puppet. These areas of assessment centered on energy in performance, projection and enunciation (when applicable), smoothness of transitions, entrances and exits.

I also ask the students to freewrite about the experience, giving them about twenty minutes to write about what worked and what didn't after the unit was finished. Their comments and suggestions really help me assess the unit and improve it from year to year.

• • •

ANOTHER APPROACH: ABSTRACT MUSIC–INSPIRED PUPPET SHOW

A really imaginative way to create a performance is to use music to inspire the students to create their own story line. There are a few things that you need to do before you meet with the students the first time.

• • •

BEFORE THE FIRST CLASS

We designed and built four large puppets (two for each class) and about two dozen smaller ones out of cardboard. We used the same method of puppet construction that was mentioned for the previous project. The large puppets were abstract shapes that had four parts. In one group of puppets, we contrasted a large puppet form with lots of jagged edges with the small puppets that were made of soft, flowing, organic lines. Another group of puppets featured a very solid-looking monolithic puppet with smaller puppets that were wispy and curved. The students would decorate them after they heard the music and had a story line.

• • •

CHOOSING THE MUSIC

We decided to use music, chosen in advance, that was fairly obscure. It was instrumental and ran about six minutes. The pieces that we chose had a lot of dynamic change. The more the music shifts around, the more likely it is that the plot will do the same. The music could be described as techno or alternative. The bands' names were Mentallo and the Fixer, the Glove, and the Legendary Pink Dots. You might want to try some alternative, classical, or New Age music. We just happened to like the dynamic sound to challenge the students' imaginations.

• • •

THE FIRST CLASS (MUSIC-INSPIRED)

A short explanation of the project—how we were going to work and what would be assessed—begins the first class. We let the students see the groupings of puppets and talk a bit about their shapes and sizes. We then ask them to close their eyes and listen to the music. After we play the music, we talk about what kinds of images they had in their heads. We divide them into two groups and each group gets one of the pieces to listen to—this time we ask them to write down story ideas for the puppet shows, keeping in mind the puppets that they have been assigned. Each group is asked to compose a rough draft of a story. They may need to argue and compromise but set a goal for the completion of the rough drafts. They can focus on the task and make decisions in a timely fashion.

• • •

WRITING THE SCRIPT (CLASSES 2–4)

The script writing usually takes a few classes. When they have a rough draft completed, the painting and decoration of the puppets begins. One year, some of the students asked to bring in found objects to hot glue to their puppets. One student took apart an old computer and used its parts for the giant puppet. Another group of students wanted one set of puppets to be black and white and another purplish pink and glitzsy. All of these wonderful ideas enhanced the story lines, which tended to be futuristic. Many of the themes had to do with acceptance of the differences of others and listening to people in authority. One even described the birth of a new race on a distant planet. I just marveled at their creativity and imagination!

• • •

REHEARSAL (CLASSES 5–9)

Once the puppets and the stories were finished, we had blocking rehearsals. We used about four class periods to refine the story lines and practice the movement of the puppets. All the groups decided to use narrators, and they were the only characters that spoke during the show. The narration was minimalistic, though, because the music was so powerful. The students wanted the music and the puppets to tell the story. One play used only four words! They were well chosen and provided insight into the story and led the audience through the experience.

• • •

THE PERFORMANCE (CLASS 10)

We performed these futuristic, absurdist pieces for the rest of the Middle School. The puppet shows challenged our audience to think and to find the meaning in a piece of performance art and drama. The performers learned that one of the purposes of theater was to make audiences think. We had discussion groups after the performances to talk about the themes. This was a wonderful part of the learning experience. My seventh grade puppeteers learned that you can't be too obscure with a theme or an audience won't get it. The audience learned to look at things in different ways—to dig for the meaning in drama and learn from it.

One of the years that we did the abstract puppet show, we were storing the giant puppets backstage for a week or two until we could get a time slot to present the show for the Lower School. The maintenance man wasn't aware of the project, and because of the abstract nature of the shapes of the puppets, he thought they were just some weird junk the drama teacher had backstage. He tossed them in a dumpster behind the theater.

The same day that this happened, my class was scheduled to rehearse the show. I went back stage and couldn't find the puppets. I called over to our Middle School head, Dr. Ebeling, and asked if he knew where they might be. He set off on the trail to discover where the giant puppets had gone while I sat with my class, improvising. About a half-hour into the class, Dr. Ebeling showed up with the puppets, a little worse for wear, but fixable. He had discovered the puppets and had climbed into the dumpster to retrieve them. The image of him rescuing our puppets from the dumpster is still vivid in my mind. He knew how important those creations were to the students and just jumped in to get them.

I learned several lessons that day. One of them was that if you are going to do an absurdist puppet show, make sure that everyone knows what the giant creatures are! Another lesson was that a supportive administrator who is willing to jump into a dumpster for the students is a friend for life!

Performing these shows for older students can be fun, too. I know that older students would have loved the music and the abstract qualities of the show. Giving your middle school students a variety of opportunities to perform for different ages and audiences is a fantastic learning experience. But make sure that they know this in advance. Some of your students will need the time to prepare for the experience and feel comfortable with it.

• • •

ASSESSMENT AND REFLECTION (CLASS 11)

The assessment and reflection are similar to that of the "Existing Story" puppet show. I also include points that have to do with script deadlines, clarity of story line, and imaginative plot. The connection between music and script is also something you might consider. How well did the story match up to the music?

It's interesting to compare the reflections of the students that participated in the "Existing Story" as opposed to those who had the "Original Story." Many students enjoyed the freedom and creativity of the invented story while others preferred the security of getting a story to illustrate. As a teacher, you'll know which approach would work best with your students.

Overall, the creativity and care that the students invest in their puppets is remarkable. This project teaches them responsibility, how to work in an ensemble, and a wide variety of ways to control large and small body movement onstage.

• • •

COMMUNITY CONNECTIONS

The first connection I'd make would be with an art teacher. Having a collaborator will make the entire project easier to handle. Don't overlook the possibilities of working with a college student on his or her break.

These puppet shows are great P.R. for your school. Taking them out to local elementary schools would be great fun, but you'd have to make sure the larger puppets fit on the bus. You might want to make connections with local libraries if you are performing existing stories.

Doing puppet shows of existing stories from language arts and social studies classes would be a wonderful possibility. Larger-than-life puppets could be used for larger-than-life characters in American literature—Johnny Appleseed, Paul Bunyon, Babe the Blue Ox, and such. You could design giant puppet shows for Black history month, Theater-in-our-Schools week or the Christmas holiday concert.

The futuristic or absurdist style puppet shows could be used to spark thematic discussions related to literature. The book, *The Giver*, comes to mind. Doing a scene from the book would involve students in a unique way. You might be able to connect with a science teacher and make the puppets resemble amoeba or protozoa. People in your school community will not be able to ignore the giant puppets. They spark enthusiasm and awe just because they are so big. At my school, we used the idea of the giant puppet show to bring the entire Middle School together in a three-day arts event that centered on building community. But that's the last chapter.

● ● ●

TIME LINE FOR THE GIANT PUPPET SHOW WITH AN EXISTING STORY

Introduction of the Lesson: Class 1
Puppet Design and Construction: Classes 2–6
Blocking and Rehearsal: Classes 7–11
Final Performance: Class 12
Assessment and Reflection: Class 13

TIME LINE FOR THE GIANT PUPPET SHOW WITH A MUSIC-INSPIRED STORY

Introduction of the Lesson: Class 1
Writing the Script: Classes 2–4
Puppet Design and Construction: Classes 5–9
Blocking and Rehearsal: Classes 10–13
Final Performance: Class 14
Assessment and Reflection: Class 15

Giant Abstract Puppets

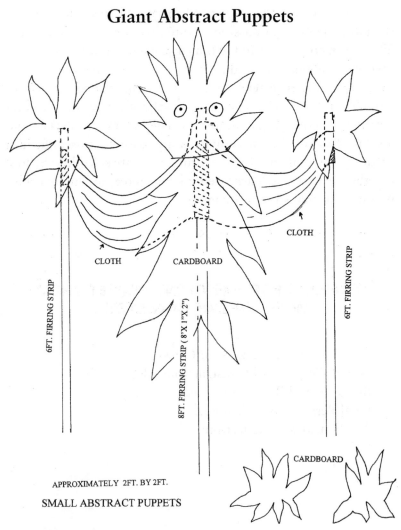

CLOTH

CLOTH

CARDBOARD

6FT. FIRRING STRIP

6FT. FIRRING STRIP

8FT. FIRRING STRIP (8"X 1"X 2")

CARDBOARD

APPROXIMATELY 2FT. BY 2FT.

SMALL ABSTRACT PUPPETS

Giant Abstract Puppets

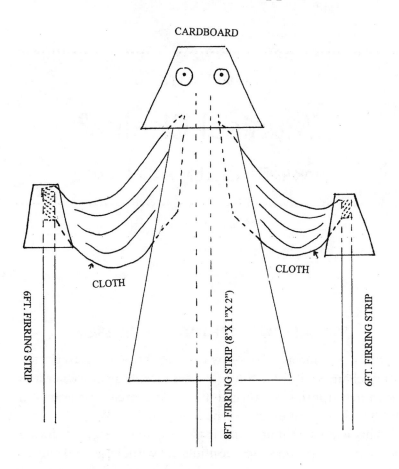

CARDBOARD

6FT. FIRRING STRIP

8FT. FIRRING STRIP (8'X 1"X 2")

6FT. FIRRING STRIP

CLOTH

CLOTH

SMALL ABSTRACT PUPPETS

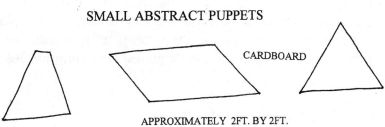

CARDBOARD

APPROXIMATELY 2FT. BY 2FT.

CHAPTER FIVE

"Musical Chairs"

GRADES SEVEN AND EIGHT

THE HISTORY BEHIND THE LESSON

I hated this game as a kid—I was never fast enough to get the empty chair. So I decided to give it a facelift as a teacher and take a new approach. I turned it into an exercise for drama in middle school—an exercise where everyone wins.

This is a short unit. I use it to keep the energy up during the year. It also develops confidence with large movement onstage and an appreciation of the talent and skill it takes to be a choreographer or dancer in musical theater. Another plus to this unit is that it uses original pieces that capture the voice of the students. Have I sufficiently piqued your curiosity? Read on!

• • •

BEFORE THE FIRST CLASS

You need a bunch of mismatched chairs. I went out to our storage barn at school and came up with a couple of kindergarten chairs, some mid-sized blocks, and a large old wooden chair. You could use any combination of "sitting devices," but you do need a minimum of three chairs. A wide variety of chairs just increase the visual quirkiness of the set.

The class should be divided into three groups of five to seven students. If your classes are larger than this configuration then you may want to do two sections…two productions rehearsing at the same time.

You also need a song. The song should be upbeat and high energy. I've used the Beatle's "Yellow Submarine" and "Octopus' Garden," Henry Mancini's "Baby Elephant Walk," and even Enya's "Sail Away." You can choose something that your students listen to, but choosing something that they aren't familiar with has its advantages. You won't hear, "I can't stand that song" and you won't have to overcome any attitude problems right from the start.

You've got the chairs. You've got the music. Now you need the script. To get the script you can do some in-class writing or you can do what I did and contact the language arts teacher. I explained to him that I needed some pieces of poetry—the best pieces that the kids had, for a production. I needed him to encourage the kids to be confident in their choices. The pieces need to be poignant, quirky, or downright funny. Most of all, they needed to be unique. He agreed to work with the students in his classes and to introduce a few poetry-writing assignments from which we could choose the perfect performance piece.

If you choose to do in-class writing, I'd start out by playing some mood music. My students loved doing this. They would lay around the stage and close their eyes and listen, and I'd tell them to go on a journey in their minds. I'd play instrumental or experimental music that wasn't too long. When the music stopped, they'd begin writing. It could be poetry or short fiction, it doesn't matter. We would do this exercise at the beginning of each class, and we soon had a wide variety of pieces to choose from. Sometimes they'd even ask their language arts teacher if they could put them in their journals to get extra credit. You could choose music around a certain theme and have them write specifically to the theme. That way you'd end up with a theme for your "Musical Chairs" production.

It is also helpful to have a video of one or two of the Monty Python Silly Walk sketches. It illustrates a point that you will be making.

Now you're ready for the first class.

• • •

THE FIRST CLASS

I begin by explaining a bit about the project to the students. I tell them that the project involves the basic concept of Musical Chairs, that is, moving onstage from one group of chairs to another in time to the music. But there are a few things added into the game. Instead of working as an individual, the students will be working in a group. Instead of a row of chairs to walk around, there are three groups of chairs to get to.

Each group is responsible for inventing a Funky Walk to get onstage and off, and to move from chair group to chair group. The groupings of chairs are arranged onstage with one grouping Stage Left, one grouping Stage Center, and one grouping Stage Right. (See drawing page 68.)

Each group will enter doing their Funky Walk to a piece of music I have chosen. They will move to a designated grouping of chairs: Stage Right, Center, or Left. When the group gets there, you will create a tableau, an arrangement of performers using levels to create an interesting picture. One of you could be sitting, one standing, one kneeling, and so forth.

Each group will be given a specific part of the music on which to enter. When all the groups have arrived at their chairs, the music will stop, and a few students will read their original poetry aloud.

When these students are finished with their readings, the music will start up again and each group will do their Funky Walk to the next group of chairs. When everyone gets to the second set of chairs, the music will stop again and more poetry readings will be given. Once more the music will start after the readings are given, and the groups will Funky Walk to the next grouping of chairs. After this last group of poetry, all the groups will do their Walk offstage and that will be the end of the show.

The diagrams at the end of this chapter should give you a clearer picture of this process. It sounds more difficult than it is. It is very helpful to run a rough rehearsal or walk through with your students at this point—concentrating only on the large movements. Don't use the music just yet. I would suggest that you group them first and then move into the performance space for a very basic walk through.

• • •

THE MUSIC AND THE FUNKY WALK
(CLASS 2)

Open the next class with the music. I've found it very effective to let the students lie on the floor and listen to the music with their eyes closed. Then I ask them to circle around and we discuss certain aspects of the music, the emotions that they felt, and the possible movement that they might do in synch with the music. Sometimes I demonstrate some possibilities. It looks pretty funny but there is method to my madness. It shows them that I am willing to look silly, to risk, to try new movements, and then to refine them for the good of the performance.

Then I send the groups to three different areas of the stage (or room) and let them experiment with movement. They tend to argue a lot, so I circulate between the groups to offer some compromises or positive reinforcement, making sure that everyone is involved in the creation process. I also answer any questions that they may have. This brainstorming/rehearsal time runs about twenty minutes. Then I ask them to sit in a circle again. I make two of the groups into an audience and have the third group present their Walk to the music. I give the other groups a chance to present, and we laugh a lot and give suggestions to each group after they present.

NOTE: At some point either before, during or after this "creating of the Funky Walk," it is most helpful to present the Monty Python Silly Walk sketches. The exaggeration and improvisation of the different types of walks spurs the kids' imaginations. Watching the video is a reflective type of activity that helps the students take a few steps back after the physicality of moving and creating the group walks. It also helps to see someone of the acting stature and popularity of John Clees or Eric Idle moving in a silly way.

When the groups return to the rehearsal of their Funky Walks, ask them to add a new movement to their routine. You can do this any number of times. You can also tell them to return to their rehearsal and make one movement larger than life or make one movement very precise and deliberate. These instructions and rehearsals will give more texture or dimension to their Walks and show them that you value the rehearsal time and the creative energy they can use to make a performance a polished piece.

• • •

THE DELIVERY OF THEIR POETRY
(CLASSES 3 AND 4)

You need a class or two to work on their scripting and the vocal part of the performance.

NOTE: I like to stagger the physical work of the Funky Walk

with the vocal work of the readings. That way we don't get bored and lose all of that wonderful middle school energy.

I ask them to pair up with a classmate and read their piece aloud. They are to write down the suggestions made by their classmates and then switch roles and be the listeners. These suggestions can be related to their energy, delivery, or their ability to project and enunciate. We then switch partners. I try to get in at least 3 switches. Then, using at least two suggestions they agree with, they read the piece onstage aloud. I comment on their changes and make a few suggestions. Once again, they get the idea that rehearsal is important and that nothing is perfect the first time through.

We then decide on an order for the performance—*who* will read *what when*. This is very important because you don't want all of the funny stuff or the serious stuff performed together. Just like the rhythm of the music and the Funky Walks, the performance needs a rhythm of its own. You arrive at this through rehearsal, trial and error, improvisation, and pure luck! It's an exciting process.

• • •

PUTTING IT ALL TOGETHER (CLASSES 5 AND 6)

The first run-through uses just the music and the Funky Walks. Call places and begin the music to get their entrance cues right. Run this a few times until they get the hang of it. Then add the movement from chair group to chair group—no dramatic readings, yet. When the students are comfortable with that, you can add the prose and poetry readings, along with the starting and stopping of the music.

As you rehearse things will seem disjointed, but they eventually come together. Cues are forgotten, people enter at the wrong time, and you may think that doing this project was a big mistake. Take heart. It gets better with each rehearsal.

The show should run like this:

MUSIC BEGINS.

> On a specific music cue, Group 1 enters Stage Right and moves to chairs Stage Left.
>
> On the second music cue, Group 2 enters Center and moves to chairs Center.
>
> On the third music cue, Group 3 enters Stage Left and moves to chairs Stage Right.

MUSIC STOPS.

> Everyone freezes except for the reader of the first piece.
>
> Then Reader 2, 3, and 4 follow. Readers should not be in the same group.

MUSIC BEGINS AGAIN.

> Group 1 moves to chairs Center.
>
> Group 2 moves to chairs Stage Right.
>
> Group 3 moves to chairs Stage Left.

MUSIC STOPS.

> Everyone freezes.
>
> Readings begin: 1, 2, 3, 4.

MUSIC BEGINS AGAIN.

> Group 1 moves to chairs Stage Right.
>
> Group 2 moves to chairs Stage Left.
>
> Group 3 moves to Center.

MUSIC STOPS.

> Everyone freezes.
>
> Readings begin: 1, 2, 3, 4.

MUSIC BEGINS AGAIN.

> Everyone exits doing their Funky Walk all the way offstage.

COSTUMING

Each group should pick a unifying element, it could be a color or a piece of clothing. (I have a great collection of funky hats!) The students should come up with the unifying factor themselves. It gives the performance an added element of ownership and identity.

• • •

PERFORMANCE (CLASS 7)

We usually performed for the whole Middle School during a designated meeting time. If your school is big, you might want to perform for one grade level. We also have performed for elementary school audiences. It would be fun to perform for parents at an Open House or an evening of curriculum review or for a teacher's meeting. Whatever the intended audience—make sure that you tell the students right from the beginning. This project/performance is usually done at a time in the school year when the kids are feeling pretty confident onstage. It's a definite "put yourself all out there" kind of experience. What with the Funky Walk and the original, "from the heart" writing, care should be taken to prepare these youngsters from the start.

• • •

ASSESSMENT

I assess the groups on only three to five points. I also assess individual students on the same points. They get a group grade and an individual grade.

An example:
1) Vocal performance
   Enunciation

Projection
Overall Delivery

2) Movement performance
Self-confidence onstage
Inventiveness/ Uniqueness of the Funky Walk
Overall polish to the performance

3) Attitude in Rehearsal
Spirit of cooperation
Persistence and diligence in rehearsal
Ability to take direction

NOTE: Make sure that the students see the grade assessment chart at the first class. They need to know up front how they will be graded.

Sometimes I assign point values to each assessment. Sometimes I just give them an Excellent, Satisfactory, or Needs Improvement. You could also use Mastery, Proficient, or Needs Improvement. Whatever works for you and your students.

• • •

REFLECTION (CLASS 8)

This part of the project is so important. I usually ask my students two questions. The questions are:

1) What worked?
2) What didn't work?

I am always amazed at the feedback from my students. They are very honest. I have learned a lot from them and refined many drama projects because of their honest suggestions. They learn lessons I never set out to teach. Reading their reflections is a truly humbling and exhilarating experience...kind of like playing Musical Chairs for the first time.

• • •

COMMUNITY CONNECTIONS

I've already mentioned the language arts connection, but there are others. The students could illustrate their poems in art and then you could take slides of the artwork and use it as a projected set. If you have a stagecraft class, the teacher could help out with a funky set design to enhance the project. The music teacher could give you suggestions for the kind of music to use. A unit of study in music may link up nicely. At our school they study the Beatles, and I have used Beatles music quite successfully for this project. You could even use "Eleanor Rigby" and have the kids share pieces about fitting in or feeling alone or being unique.

• • •

TIME LINE FOR "MUSICAL CHAIRS"

Introducing the Project/Walk Through: Class 1
Introducing the Music and Inventing the Funky Walks: Class 2
The Delivery of the Poetry: Classes 3 and 4
Putting It All Together: Classes 5 and 6
Performance: Class 7
Reflection/Assessment: Class 8

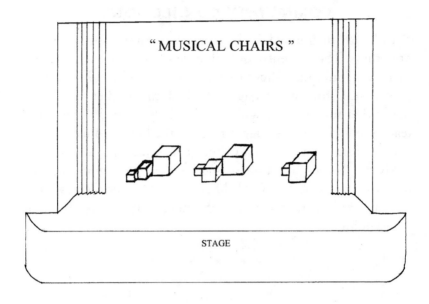

"MUSICAL CHAIRS"

STAGE

TOP VIEW

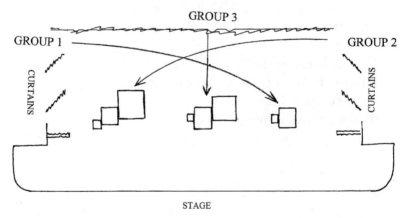

GROUP 3

GROUP 1

GROUP 2

CURTAINS

CURTAINS

STAGE

CHAPTER SIX

Rock 'n' Roll Playwriting

GRADE EIGHT

THE HISTORY BEHIND THE LESSON

I was driving somewhere listening to an oldies station. A song came on. I think it was "Tell Laura I Love Her" or "Teen Angel." I asked myself, "I wonder what happened to these characters before this song? I wonder what will happen *after?*"

Then, being the drama teacher I am, I started to imagine how I could use this idea with my middle school students. They loved the oldies—songs from the 50s and 60s. Our music teacher, Marilyn Crooker, loved teaching these songs. All the elements were there for a drama project, so I talked to Marilyn and we began to get our ideas down on paper.

The students would work in groups and listen to two songs that we chose in advance. Then they choose one of the songs that they liked the best to use for their final project. We usually gave them one upbeat song and one ballad. The characters in the song would be the primary cast. The groups write down the words of the song or find them on the Internet. The main conflict and a short summary of the story of the song are noted.

Then the students brainstorm for ideas as to what might have taken place before and after the song. They would, in effect, create a scene from a musical, embedding the song in it. The students memorize and block the scenes and the song in drama class and learn how to sing the song in music class, performing the final polished piece for the school's spring concert in March.

NOTE: This workshop doesn't need to be such a huge production. I had the cooperation of a colleague who made it a wonderful collaborative effort. In recent years, I taught this workshop alone and had the students lip-synch the songs. It works either way. We chose to perform for a spring concert. These musical playlets could be done as an in-class project, too.

• • •

BEFORE THE FIRST CLASS

The first thing to do in preparation is to choose the music and group the students. If the songs are going to be performed as a polished piece in a musical concert, then the music teacher should have a say in the group formation, making sure that you have at least one strong vocal talent in each group.

Each group gets two songs to listen to. Keep in mind that the songs you choose should have a strong story line. Songs like "Splish, Splash," "Are You Lonesome Tonight?," "Mr. Sandman," "Get a Job," "Leader of the Pack," "Rock Around the Clock," and "Yakety Yak" are great. I've also used teenage tragedy songs like "Teen Angel" and "Tell Laura I Love Her." The scenes border on melodrama and farce.

I needed three CD players, one for each group, so that they could play the song over and over again as they blocked. I also rented a variety of videos to show them some examples of scenes that led into and out of songs. During one of the very first classes the students watch these lead-in scenes, songs, and lead-out scenes and come up with a list of elements they want to include in their performances. I've used examples from *Fiddler on the Roof, Little Shop of Horrors, Grease, Bye, Bye Birdie, Beauty and the Beast, Nightmare Before Christmas,* and *Music Man.*

Preparation for costuming can be as complex or as simple as you wish. Some years I have asked parents to clean out their closets. Lots of 60s and 70s clothes—from bell-bottoms to Hawaiian shirts—were donated to our stash of costumes. Some years I have haunted our local secondhand stores on dollar-a-bag days. Garage sales and church- or school-sponsored rummage sales are also a great source of costumes.

If you are working collaboratively with a music specialist, it is a good idea to have a few meetings to decide on a schedule, complete with deadlines. Good communication with your colleague will help the workshop run smoothly. If your students take more time blocking or memorizing the songs, you can talk to your colleague immediately and adjust the schedule. It is extremely helpful to have a few joint rehearsals and a dress rehearsal with both teachers present. If there are changes to be made, then you can give these notes to the students or even ask each other for advice on how a particular point can be improved.

I was fortunate to have a fantastic working relationship with our music teacher. We had been partners working on the upper school musical for years, and we both taught in the middle school. We checked in with each other almost every day, filling each other in on where the students were in regard to the schedule. We arranged a dress rehearsal the day before the concert with the full support of the other teachers. It was a great situation because they saw the value of the arts program and what it did for the students.

• • •

THE FIRST CLASS

A general explanation of the workshop is given for the opening class. I usually begin by playing a song that we are not going to use and then ask them some questions to start a discussion that leads into an explanation of the project. It usually goes something like this—

I play "Mr. Sandman," recorded in 1954 by the Chordettes, and I ask the following questions:

1) Where does this song take place? What time of day?
2) What do we know about the characters in this song? Do any of them have names? Can you come up with some words or phrases that describe them?
3) What might have happened before this song took place? What events could have led to the singing of this song? Where would the scene preceding the song have taken place?
4) What do the characters want? Is there a conflict with what they want and what the other characters want? Can you think of possible conflicting objectives that these characters might have?
5) What is the main idea or theme of this song?
6) What do you think happens when this song is over? How could the conflict be resolved in this last scene? Where would this scene take place?
7) Can you add extra characters? What would their names be?

These questions lead to a variety of discussions. I bring the class to an end by telling them that they are going to take a song much like "Mr. Sandman" and write a scene leading into the song and another scene to act out after the song is finished. I make a copy of the questions that have led to this discussion to give them for their analysis of the song that their group choses to do.

• • •

WATCHING THE VIDEOS (CLASS 2)

To learn from the masters of the American musical, I take a class period to watch some examples of lead-in scenes, songs, and the scenes following a song to compile a list of elements. These elements are the building blocks of the scenes that the students will eventually write. They include:

1) How do character introductions and exposition occur
2) Working with a time limit (most scenes go by very fast but include a lot of information)
3) The introduction of the main conflict
4) The use of props as clues to characters
5) How to construct lively dialogue
6) Types of acting styles

Now the students have a set of questions and a set of elements to guide them as they work on this project. The next step is to get them into groups, give them their songs, and a list of deadlines for the workshop.

• • •

THE SONGS (CLASS 3)

Each group gets two songs. This gives them a chance to evaluate the songs and choose the one that they find the most exciting and has the most possibilities for turning into a scene. I give them a CD player and the songs, and they go to a part of the stage or the room to listen to these songs. They discuss which songs have the most potential. Then they chose one song around which their opening and closing scene is constructed.

I usually have three groups of students per class. All the songs are from a certain era. One year we chose only surfing and California songs, and the kids had a blast. They chose to perform "Surfin' Safari," "California Dreaming," and

"California Girls." We wove all of the scenes together, connected by the theme of traveling from Ohio to California in a psychedelic van.

One year we chose Teenage Tragedies from the 50s and their scenes were melodramatic. Another year we had a random mix from the 50s. Their choices were "Splish Splash," "Sandman," "Are You Lonesome Tonight?," and "Leader of the Pack." Every year the students' choices really surprised us. Giving them a choice is important because they have to live with this song a long time. The students also feel more invested in the project when they've had a voice in some of the choices.

Here is an example of what a group of students can do with some of the preliminaries. One year we used "Mr. Sandman." The kids came up with three sets:

1) A street with the characters walking home from school
2) A bedroom where a slumber party was taking place and where the song is sung
3) A malt shop where the last scene is played out

There were seven students in a group, and they decided that they would have three girls, three guys, and one sandman. The discussion in the first scene had to do with the prom and who wanted to go with whom. The conflict was that the girls didn't know if the guys even knew that they existed. The slumber party was another scene that showed how much the girls wanted to go with these particular guys, and then the song was sung as they begged Mr. Sandman to bring them a "dream." They fall asleep and the Sandman brings a boy for each girl in a short dream sequence. Then the last scene takes place in a malt shop where the Sandman has turned into a soda jerk and is responsible for bringing the girls together with the boys from their dreams. To arrive at this clever group of scenes required compromising, concentrated effort, a lot of work, and a basic knowledge of how to construct the scene.

Once they have made the choice of a song, they listen to their song quietly. One student acts as the secretary, keeping everything together in a folder that I give them. Their first goal is to listen to the song two or three times and answer the list of questions we compiled in the first class. Then, after they have discussed the answers to the questions, they should dicuss the list of elements. I also remind them that an audience wants to be entertained so they should keep this in mind. If they are having fun onstage, the audience will be drawn into the scene.

● ● ●

PLAYWRITING TIME OUT (CLASSES 4 AND 5)

At this point, you might want to take some time out to talk about playwriting format and scene construction. Examining some existing plays or musicals for examples of character and set description, stage directions, plot synopsis, and so on will familiarize your students with the format. Pass out a few examples of scripts and have the students examine them. Most students have seen a play before and are familiar with the format to use. But you might be surprised how many middle school students don't understand the meaning of "At rise" or don't know that you have to put stage directions in parentheses.

This Playwriting Time Out is not an in-depth study of playwriting but just meant to give the students some familiarity with how a musical script is constructed. The scenes that my middle school students came up with were easy to follow and a lot of fun to watch. The emphasis in doing this project is not to produce an incredible libretto but to learn some of the basic concepts of musical theater.

I also emphasize the importance of a good story line and conflicting objectives. Circulating between the groups as they are writing their scenes, I reinforce these two points until the students start to recite, when they see me coming, "We know, Mrs. J. A good story has a beginning, middle, and end."

CONSTRUCTING THE SCENES (CLASSES 6–8)

Constructing the scenes that lead in and out of the songs takes up the next few classes. I circulate from group to group to help and offer possibilities if they reach a standstill. A part must be written for every member of the group. Smaller parts can be written for shy students. I step in and remind them that our set capabilities are limited when they decide to have three complex settings such as a malt shop, a car garage, and a frilly bedroom complete with vanity dressing table! We can do a minimalist set with a few set pieces. We also have a set of blocks of varying sizes that can be used for just about anything.

I set a goal for each group at the beginning of each class. One person checks in with me and we decide what can be accomplished during the class period. This gives the students a chance to work at their own pace while giving me a chance to see if they are wasting time or running into problems. I also keep track in my grade book whether they complete their planned goal. This day-to-day assessment is factored into their final grade. A final draft of the script, with copies for each student in their group and the teacher, is the final goal of this series of classes. The script should be double-spaced for the changes that will be made in rehearsal.

• • •

THE REHEARSAL (CLASSES 9–12)

BLOCKING THE SCENES

If your students are not familiar with blocking a scene, take time now to give them some of the basics. You can do this in any number of ways. One choice would be to present a scene that you block while they watch. This should not be one of their scenes. They need a sense of ownership with their work: It creates too many problems if a teacher chooses one of their scenes to block. You can find many plays that are short and perfect for using as examples printed in *Plays* magazine, published by Plays, Inc.

Another choice is to circulate from group to group giving some pointers as the students block. I have had to really watch myself as I circulate, reminding myself that I am not directing—and I end up asking a lot of questions to help lead the students to an understanding of the dramatic process of blocking. Nothing will kill the enthusiasm and energy more than a teacher walking over to a group and spending an entire period blocking their scene. But, there are times when the students are really at a loss as to what to do to solve a problem with staging the scene. When offering suggestions, I give them several possibilities so that the students have a choice. Sometimes this amounts to "Watch your back" when a student has his back turned to the audience, and sometimes it involves talking to the entire group about a specific script revision that they do not see as part of the problem.

• • •

BLOCKING THE SONGS

This is unfamiliar territory to most students. Blocking a play is one thing, but blocking a song is quite another matter. I am always surprised at what the students come up with. They use back up groups to doo-wop their way through the song. They ask about 50s and 60s dance moves and add dances to their songs. I circulate nonstop during these rehearsals asking questions like, "Where do you want the audience to focus its attention?" "Would you like me to take a look at what you have?" and reinforce things like, "Less is more" and "Use the space."

• • •

DRESS REHEARSAL (CLASS 13)

Once the scene and the songs are blocked, the students perform a dress rehearsal. I give them a "first look" assessment based on a variety of dramatic points. I also give them a grade on their script writing. If they decide to refine their script, then their grade goes up.

Costumes can be simple or complex. If parents or grandparents can donate some vintage 50s and 60s clothes, a connection is made between generations. It is possible with all of the revivals during the past years to get bell-bottoms, paisley shirts, and leather jackets. The rule of thumb is the wilder, the better. We started a costume collection with the donations. Then a parent who could sew made us a set of 50s poodle skirts that we still use. By the time the dress rehearsal came around, it had turned into a real community effort.

• • •

FINAL PERFORMANCE (CLASS 14)

As I mentioned previously, my classes presented their final performance at our spring concert. Having an audience of parents and friends was a wonderful experience. The praise that the students received for their originality and enthusiasm, their creative costuming, and their set designs boosted their self-confidence and pride in their dramatic ability.

• • •

REFLECTION AND ASSESSMENT (CLASS 15)

A teacher who has been consistent with the check-in system and goal setting and completion established at the beginning of the process already has a day-to-day accounting of the work done by each group. Add in the script grade, the "first-look" dress rehearsal and the grade given for the final performance, and you have an assessment of process and product. I also add an individual grade for the final performance based on performance values like projection, enunciation, and self-confidence on stage. The group grade is then averaged with the individual grade and that is the final grade that the students receive. They also get an effort grade on our report cards.

I have someone videotape the performance, and we watch the tape together. I usually make an in-school cast party out of it, bringing cookies and pop to celebrate. I ask them to take some time, ten minutes or so, to write up commendations and recommendations for them and for me. These reflections are multipurposed. First, the *real* learning takes place upon reflection. I firmly believe that when a student learns to take time out to think back on a dramatic experience, they make connections and gain deeper understanding. Second, I gain such insight into the process of the lesson. Every year I change my lessons because of the feedback that I receive from the students. Just as the students grow in their knowledge and experiences of drama, I grow in the knowledge of the many ways to teach it.

● ● ●

COMMUNITY CONNECTIONS

The most obvious community connection is related to audience. Because of the simple sets, minimalistic costuming, and music on a portable CD, it would be very easy to tour these scenes to local elementary schools. Nursing homes or retirement communities also present audience possibilities. Parent evenings at the school or even all-school fairs can be enlivened by a performance from the fifties or the sixties.

I remember one year we had an extremely quiet and shy youngster who broke out in song with "Are You Lonesome Tonight?" The audience was so appreciative of his beautiful voice they raved about his performance. This same youngster went on to join an upper school quartet, to play the lead in *Godspell* when he was a senior, and to sing in a college quartet.

If you have a dance specialist or, luckier yet, dance classes for your students, you could ask them to collaborate with you to refine the choreography of the musical numbers. Asking a local college or community theater choreographer to come in as a guest speaker would help spark ideas for your students.

A connection with a music teacher really strengthens the whole project. Having the students sing the songs is the best possible experience. It gives them a profound respect for musical theater, its performers, directors, and choreographers.

Connections with other disciplines are also possible. The year that we used all California songs, they could have been done in conjunction with a unit in social studies about the history of California. The teenage tragedy songs could be used to connect the language arts class and the themes of some of today's young adult literature. Connecting it to science conjures up visions of a backup group in lab coats, but it's a bit of a stretch.

This unit is so much fun to do. We still hear from alums about the experience and how great it was to get onstage and sing the oldies. The scenes that the students come up with are imaginative and answer the original question I asked myself while driving in the car that day. "I wonder what happened to these characters before this song? I wonder what will happen *after?*"

• • •

TIME LINE FOR ROCK 'N' ROLL PLAYWRITING

Introduction and Listening Exercises: Class 1
Studying Classic Musical Theater Songs: Class 2
Song Analysis: Class 3
Playwriting Time Out: Classes 4–5
Constructing the Scenes: Classes 6–8
Rehearsal: Classes 9–12
Dress Rehearsal: Class 13
Final Performance: Class 14
Assessment and Reflection: Class 15

CHAPTER SEVEN

Community Building Days

GRADES SIX, SEVEN, AND EIGHT

THE HISTORY BEHIND THE PROJECT

Each year during September, our middle school runs an event called Community Building Days. This event usually runs from three to five days. Classes are not held, and the time is devoted to developing a healthy community spirit that starts the school year on a positive note. Given the times in which we live and the tragedies we read about in the news, it is a great idea that helps the students form bonds of friendship between grade levels (6, 7, and 8) and gives the teachers a chance to interact with students outside of a classroom situation.

For many years, the three days centered on outdoor experiences that strengthened ties between the students, culminating with one day of canoeing. One year there was a camp-out on campus, another year outdoor games were played that helped youngsters develop trust in one another. But every year the emphasis was on outdoor activities. This approach was a big hit with some of the students, but others felt lost or left out if they didn't excel at physical education.

The idea for an arts-centered project came to me as I sat in a meeting. The faculty was being asked to do some out-of-the-box thinking about Community Building Days. The students coming into the middle school had been to a wide variety of camps in previous years, and they had played many of the games that we relied on to build community. We needed to design a new and exciting three-day experience that would engage our students and enliven our faculty volunteers.

I mentioned that there was nothing like a play to build community. Everyone pulls together to get a production onstage. I suggested that we should try an arts-centered approach. Every student would be involved in the creation of the production, from playwriting to technical assistance, from building the set to performing onstage. We could still play some outdoor games scattered throughout the day, games that would concentrate on cooperation and working toward a goal. But the main emphasis would be on the creation and performance of a community-produced production. The faculty was intrigued by the possibilities. Dr. Ebeling, our Middle School Head at the time, said that I should go ahead and develop the idea for discussion at the next faculty meeting.

Developing a program that keeps an entire middle school busy over a three-day period was daunting. I needed the support of my fine arts colleagues in middle school, as well as the entire faculty, who would need to be given crystal clear plans for running such a project. I set up a system of communication through inter-office memos to make sure that I was in touch with the people whose support was crucial to the implementation of this experience.

Over the next few months, I worked on a plan to present to the faculty. It had to involve every student in a wide variety of exercises that would eventually lead to a final production. The Giant Puppet Shows had been such a big hit with the middle school that I zeroed in on this idea. I grouped the Middle School students across grade levels and assigned one faculty advisor to each group. I then worked on a packet of exercises and instructions for the advisor. These packets had to be organized and explanations had to be clearly understood by teachers who did not have a background in the fine arts.

The teachers in the middle school were totally supportive, and I got special support from the other fine arts teachers in the division. The art teacher offered to do sidewalk chalk drawing, and the music teacher offered to do found-object musical instruments that could be used in the performances. P.E. teachers offered to do community building games at several times during the day and to take care of all the equipment that might be needed. I presented the plan and the faculty voted to give it a try.

During the following months I held workshop sessions to show my colleagues how to run sessions of improvisational exercises that would serve as icebreakers and idea generators. At these meetings we also went over every step of every day. The preparation we did for these three days really helped the whole project run smoothly.

What follows in this chapter is the day-by-day guide that we followed for Community Building Days at the beginning of the school year. This entire three-day experience is worth all of the time and effort it took to plan and implement it. In this day and age, when schools are searching for ways to heal the rift between groups of middle school students, an arts-centered experience not only makes sense, it makes a difference.

Dr. Ebeling puts it quite eloquently in the following paragraph:

> Children learn from those they love. And Community Building Days are mainly about laying the groundwork for people to feel the safety that comes from being loved. When children feel known, understood, and respected (in a word, loved) by those around them, they feel free to take risks: emotional,

intellectual, and artistic risks that are the crucible of creativity. If our children aren't creating, then we should close up shop. Because it is through the creative process that our children move us all beyond what is to what might be. And through Community Building Days we all learn about what might be.

This is an abbreviated version of the schedule that we followed for Community Building Days. You can decide how it would work for your school and add or subtract as you see fit. I will be shortening the term Community Building Days to CBD for the majority of this description.

• • •

Community Building Days
THE WORLD THAT
WE CAN CREATE

DAY 1
MEETING AND SCRIPTING

8:25–9:00: Middle school meets in auditorium. Short explanation of the activities that will take place during the next three days. Break into CBD groups and go to individual classrooms.

9–10:15: First Activity.
 Part one: Introduction/Improvs
 Part two: Artifact from the future
 Part three: Prompts and written reflection

10:15–11:00: Music and Listening Activity

11:00–12:00: Play break with Outdoor Activity

12–12:45: Lunch

12:45–1:00: Return to auditorium for an explanation of chalk mural activity

1:00–1:40: Sidewalk Chalk Mural

1:40–2:30: Return to your classrooms for the next session. Scripting

2:30–3:15: Play break; Outdoor Games by the P.E. Dept.

3:15–3:25: Return to Auditorium. Remind students to bring in found-object instrument for day two

DAY 2
REFINING THE SCRIPT AND CONSTRUCTION OF PUPPETS

8:25–8:45: Meet in auditorium. Assemble in CBD groups

8:45–10:00: Go to your CBD classrooms; refine and edit the script

10:00–10:40: Continue Sidewalk Chalk Mural

10:45–12:00: Begin construction of puppets

12:00–12:45: Lunch

12:45–1:00: Meet in auditorium to give a progress report.

1:00–2:00: Go to classrooms. Finish puppet construction. Clean up. Rehearse with puppets and refine the script.

2:00–2:30: Return to auditorium. Bring found-object instruments

2:30–3:20: Return to CBD classrooms to add found-object instrumentation to your scripts

DAY 3
REHEARSAL AND PERFORMANCE

8:25–8:45: Meet in auditorium

8:45–9:30: Rehearse in CBD classrooms

9:30–11:50: Groups pair up for rehearsal in the auditorium

11:50–12:35: Lunch

12:35: Return to auditorium for setup

1:00–3:00: Performance

3:00–3:25: Refreshments and cleanup

• • •

Community Building Days
THE WORLD THAT
WE CAN CREATE

DAY 1
MEETING AND SCRIPTING

The entire middle school met in the auditorium at 8:25 for an explanation of what was going to happen during the next three days. The explanation should be brief. If you have enlisted the aid of colleagues to run some of the activities, then you should allow them to take some of the time for a short explanation.

My fine arts colleagues offered to do mini-workshops in their fields of music and art. Mrs. Crooker, the music teacher, was in charge of explaining how the students could make instruments out of found objects. She demonstrated several examples and told the students that they would be required to bring in an object that could be used as a musical instrument. Mr. Fouts, the art teacher, was in charge of a huge sidewalk mural that the students would draw outside. The subject of the mural would be the theme of Community Building Days, *The World that We Can Create*. Each group would be given a section of the walkway to fill with drawings and an assortment of chalk with which to color. The students would work on the chalk drawing for several days, adding to it each time. He was also in charge of helping each group make banners to celebrate their story. This banner was actually a type of back up in case it rained and we were unable to make the sidewalk chalk mural.

After my fine arts colleagues explained their activities we broke into CBD groups and went to individual rooms. The CBD groups were decided in advance enlisting the help of the Middle School teachers. We mixed the grade levels within the groups.

There were sixth, seventh, and eighth graders in every group. This was also helpful in the puppet construction and the improvisational games because the eighth graders had done these activities before in my drama classes.

INTRODUCTION/IMPROVS

To start the groups off, we began with some "icebreakers," some improvisational games that would introduce the students to each other. Each teacher had done these improvs with me in a workshop prior to Community Building Days so they knew what they were doing. I moved from group to group helping out when I thought it might be necessary. I did this a lot in the next three days, and the teachers told me afterward that it was really comforting to have me looking in on them.

An explanation of the improvisational games that we used follows. You can also use other kinds of improvisations. I used some from the "Young Playwrights, Inc." curriculum (an excellent resource) and a variety of other improv books that I have.

TOSS THE NERF

Objective: To learn the names of the people in your group by developing and reinforcing the powers of concentration. To break the ice within a group through physical activity and to help students take some risks in front of a small group.

Procedure: "Everyone has played catch. Here is an exercise that uses the game of catch with a twist. I have a Nerf ball here and I'm going to toss it to a student as I call his or her name. The idea is to toss the ball so that the person is able to catch it. We must also establish a pattern and stick to it. If I throw to Greg, then I will always throw to Greg. Greg will always throw to Jonell, and so on. Let's try one round.

"Now we are going to add something. Let's try to use our voices in different ways. As we call each other's names, let's use different inflections each time. Try to experiment with some unique tones of voice or projection or whatever.

"Let's try a few rounds.

"Now we are going to add something. Remembering to keep the pattern, let's walk around the space and play. Take it slowly for the first round and remember that this is a game of CATCH not DROP! Locate your "catcher" and toss the ball but keep moving! 'Let's try a round.'"

The leader then tries subsequent rounds reminding students to add inflection: keep moving; go faster; try different ways to toss the Nerf.

COP AND THIEF

Objective: By relying on our listening ability, conflicting objectives can be resolved. Concentration and group cooperation are essential to this improv exercise.

Procedure: "Some of you have played this game before but I would like you to listen carefully to the rules once again.

"One person will play the Cop and one, the Thief. The cop's objective is to catch the thief before the jewels are found. The thief's objective is to find the jewels before the cop catches him or her. Both are blindfolded.

"The rest of the group will need to form a circle that is the boundary for the game. If a cop or thief comes near the edge of the boundary, then GENTLY and QUIETLY guide them back into the circle. (Key word here is GENTLY!!) The circle people are mute, and they must maintain silence for the success of the game. Even when you are bursting with laughter, you must concentrate and control it! When one of the objectives is achieved, then you can talk.

"O.K. I need four people; two to play cop and thief, and

two to tie on the blindfold and turn them SILENTLY and disorient them. The cop and thief cannot talk once the blindfold is on. I also need one person to hide the jewels (keys) on the floor within the circle. O.K. we need quiet. Let's begin."

Everyone will clamor to play this game. I usually let the "Disorientors" become the cop and thief next. I will also try to have the blindfolds a certain color for the cop and thief to help the observers as they watch. (I use black for the cop and red for the thief.) Try to give everyone a chance to play both roles. If it gets too rowdy, I have them sit and talk a bit about how important listening is to the success of the game. Also, some kids try to make noise to draw the players off of their objective. This is detrimental to the game, so I stop and try to explain that the rules have to be followed or the exercise will fail. The cop and thief will come up with a variety of different ways to achieve their objective. This is great. You might want to have everyone sit down after half of the class has gone and discuss what is working or what it was like to play cop or thief. Discussion of how the entire group contributes to the success of the game is vital. You can ask questions like, "How does listening enter into the exercise? What does each character do to achieve their objectives?"

ARTIFACT FROM THE FUTURE

This exercise helps the students start thinking creatively. It is a lot of fun and led beautifully into the third activity of the day.

The artifacts were simple objects that I had collected like plastic cup holders, small Wiffle balls, paper clips, and Velcro pieces. The following paragraph is a script of what you say to begin the game. The group is seated in a circle as you read to them.

The year is 2050. Scientists (you!) have finally figured out how to send things into the future and to receive artifacts from the future. Each group has an artifact that has been sent back from the future. There is some disagreement as to the nature of the object, and you are here to convince your fellow scientists that your theory is the correct one. Take a moment to pass the artifact around the circle. Think of the type of people who would use the object, what they would use it for, what it might tell us of the society of the future. Now share your theory with your fellow scientists.

This exercise is actually an improv in which each student, while sitting in a circle, takes the object and says, "I know what this is…" and begins a wild explanation of what they think the object might be. The next student takes the object and says, "No. That's not what it is. It is…" and they begin their story. It is a wonderful, imaginative exercise that gets the students in the mind-set for the next exercise. You can begin the improvisation, and the students can model your behavior. After everyone has a chance to talk, you say the following:

Take a minute to think. If you were to send one artifact into the future, what would you send and why? Remember that this object would represent your personal hopes, dreams, likes, or dislikes to the people of the future. Share with the group.

Once again you direct the discussion around the circle as everyone contributes. Sometimes the students will be reluctant to be honest and talk about a funny or silly artifact. You can handle this in a variety of different ways, but getting them to speak truthfully and sincerely should be your goal. This exercise works on many levels. It starts a thought process about a world in the future that they can create, which is the theme of CBD. It also helps the students to begin understanding each other and knowing each other on a deeper level.

This next activity is centered around the following prompts. The teachers who led the discussions were surprised when they ran out of time! You can begin with the first prompt and work your way through the last ones. When you discuss the following statements, ask for examples from movies, TV shows, and songs that the students have seen and heard.

Prompts:
1) The future will be run by machines and technology. Do you agree or disagree?
2) Some people say that this is the beginning of a "new age": new music, philosophy, spiritual life, kindness to others... and so on, in which mankind will become a family linked by technological advances. What do you think?
3) Some people say that violence will consume our cities, and criminals will overthrow the government. What do you think?
4) Others say that aliens will help us with our problems or take over our cities and minds. Have you seen any movies that illustrate this view of the future?

After a lively discussion, ask the students to write the answers to the following questions. The reason that we had the students write their responses first and then discuss them is that some middle school students will simply repeat what their friends have said and not give themselves time to think about what *they* think. By writing their responses down first, the students were given time to reflect on the questions and come up with original answers. After writing for each question, the students should discuss their answers and then move to the next question.

1) If you could build your future world, what would you include in your world?
2) How do you envision specific institutions? Schools? Families and Friends? Social Life?
3) What are your hopes and dreams for your future?

After these discussions, it is time to listen to the music.

MUSICAL IMAGININGS AND DISCUSSIONS

I had chosen and taped two selections of music for each group beforehand. Each group got one tape; all the selections were different. The music we used was futuristic, some of the selections coming from video games. We tried to find music that changed several times during the selection so that the students' imaginations would be challenged when thinking of a story as they listened to their selections. Each group had a tape recorder to listen to the tape. I asked the teachers to make sure that they took some notes on the music-inspired stories that the students told. The note taking helps when the group, while writing their scripts, hits a creative dry spell. You can refer to your notes and make suggestions to help the students.

Before you play the music, tell the students:

Close your eyes and listen to this piece of music...While you are listening, imagine a story about the future. Be ready to share the story when the music ends.

Then play the first selection of music. When the music selection is finished, tell the students:

Let's go around the circle and share the stories we saw in our heads.

This is when you should take notes on the stories. These

notes should record any story lines that you think could be used for the final script. You will be surprised at the concentration the youngsters show during the music and imagining part of the process. The kids LOVE this part. Then you repeat this process with the second piece of music.

After they share their second story, you should ask the group the following questions:

1) Which story did you like the best?
2) Which story would make a good dramatic presentation about the future?
3) Can we include some of your ideas from the discussion that we had earlier? What kind of characters could act out this story?
4) What would they be like?
5) Can you describe them?
6) Which musical selection did you like the best?

You should get the students to go beyond the surface, to a deeper level. Guide them toward a story that combines hopes, dreams, and positive changes.

Take notes on what they like the best: This will be the basis for their script. When you get back together after lunch, you will be writing the script from these notes. You will be using one piece of music to introduce the production and the other one to close the production.

PLAY BREAK

These play breaks were scattered throughout the three days. They usually involved some outside activity, like explosion tag, capture the flag, and spud. The physical activity helped to balance all the classroom work we were doing. The physical education department handled this part of the day, giving the CBD teachers a break. After about forty minutes of game playing, we went to lunch. Lunch lasted for forty minutes.

CHALK DRAWING

After lunch everyone returned to the auditorium for a detailed explanation of the outside chalk drawing. Each group was given a section of sidewalk on which to draw pictures about their hopes and dreams for the future. The weather cooperated while we were making the chalk mural, but there is always the banner activity that can be used as a substitute. It would be smart to check a three-day forecast to make sure that you have good weather for all of the days unless you don't mind having the chalk drawing erased by rain and having the students begin again. The sidewalk art surrounded the entire Middle School, where the Lower and Upper School students could all enjoy looking at it. The artwork generated a lot of excitement.

After about forty-five minutes of chalk drawing, the students returned to their classrooms for the next session.

SCRIPTING

You begin by asking the students to sit in a circle. Then you say:

> From your writings and all of your morning discussions, write a script with a narrator, that takes place in a future world of possibilities and promise. I will write the necessary elements you must include in your script on the board. You will be working in the groups in which you were placed on the first day.

Then write the following on the board:
1) Everyone must have a part and everyone should help with the writing of the script.
2) Keep in mind that the characters in the play will be one very large puppet (run by three people), and the other characters will be smaller puppets cut out of cardboard.
3) One person will have to run the music.
4) Some people will have to be part of the Band.

5) The show can only run between seven and ten minutes.

6) You must use one of the pieces of music as an introduction and one as an ending. This sets the mood for your script and signals to the other groups that the play is over.

When you break it down, you need students for:

1 narrator

3 large, puppet people who manipulate the giant puppet

1 music technician to run the music

2 or 3 Band members

The rest of your group will be the puppeteers for the smaller puppets.

Make sure you remind them to remember the essentials of a good dramatic story:

• Characters that you can sympathize with
• A strong beginning, middle, and end
• Lively characters and believable dialogue
• A clear theme or lesson to the story
• A positive conflict resolution

This activity usually takes an hour. You should write down all of the great brainstorming ideas that are bound to be discussed as the students write the story. You can use them as a resource in case they hit a snag in the story writing. As the students discuss who will do what, make sure that these assignments are fair and equitable. Some students will naturally gravitate to the non-performing roles. But you need to know your kids and when to step in when you think that someone is being pushed in a certain direction by the group. You also need to remember that this is their script, stepping in only when they really have hit an impasse. You will have to work fast and really get them to work together as a group. Don't let them spend a lot of time bickering. Keep them focused and explain that because of the time limit you need to have a script completed by the end of this forty-minute session. It IS possible when you think that the length of the play is only ten minutes, but it will be challenging to get the whole story told in that amount of time. The play/puppet show can take any form...poetic, mythical, folktale, even pantomime! Help them discover a creative way to present the play.

As they near script completion, have someone sketch out what the characters might look like and how you might translate these into three-dimensional puppets. Keep all of this, including the rough draft of the script, which is the ultimate goal of the session.

After this session, we had another outdoor activity and then met in the auditorium for the last ten minutes of the day. At this meeting, it is important to remind students to bring in a found-object instrument for the second day. Reminding the students about this homework right before they go home helps them to remember. In spite of this reminder, some students did forget their instruments the next day, but we made sure that we had a few extras, like some empty two-liter bottles and jars of dried beans, for them to use.

DAY 2

We met first in the auditorium to get the students into their CBD groups. Then the groups went to their classrooms to begin refining and editing the script. We took an hour and fifteen minutes for this first session. This appears to be a long time for working on the script, but it flew by.

Remember to remind the students of the list of "must-haves" that you wrote on the board yesterday. When you think that you have a final draft, have a few read-throughs of the script to see if you need to make any changes. It should run at least seven to ten minutes. Have a couple of students work on and refine the sketches of the puppets that they began yesterday.

CHALK DRAWING

The next activity of the day was to return to the giant mural in chalk that we had begun the previous day. We took about thirty minutes to do this, but you can decide how long you want to give to this. We did have a backup plan in case it rained. Each group had a large banner that they were to make for their group to use as we paraded into the auditorium for the final performance. The banners were to be constructed inside the classrooms while it was raining, but fortunately, we had sunny weather and never had to resort to banner creation.

THE CONSTRUCTION OF THE PUPPETS

After the session of chalk drawing, we began to make the large and small puppets in the classrooms. The puppets we made were exactly like the ones from the Giant Puppet shows. The drawings of these larger-than-life puppets can be seen in chapter four.

The construction time frame will be different for each group. You may need more time to refine the script and sketch the puppets, then begin working on construction. Perhaps you will begin immediately working on construction. It is not unusual to use an entire morning, from nine until noon, constructing puppets. The key word is adaptability! You can get a sense from your group when they need a break or when they should stop working on the script and begin construction. In each group there were eighth grade students who had previous experience with puppet construction; the teachers used their expertise to help move the process along. I circulated from group to group, offering my help whenever or wherever possible. To see their ideas take shape in such a BIG way was remarkable. One group decided to make a robot puppet and used aluminum foil to decorate it. One group made a huge chameleon because they felt that the future belonged to a race of creatures that could adapt and change!

A WORD ABOUT CONSTRUCTION MATERIALS

We tried to keep the materials for construction simple. We didn't want to be cleaning up a lot of messy paints and such. Some of the groups did use hot glue guns and found objects to decorate their puppets, but an adult supervisor watched the use of these items in the group. If you want to use some of the materials that we shied away from, feel free to do whatever fits your group.

In general, each CBD group should have the following materials:
- Large, white cardboard
- Large and small markers
- Pencils, regular and colored
- Three 4-foot-tall 1 x 2s. This wood is needed for each of the large puppets (3 pieces of wood: one for the body and two for the hands)
- Duct tape
- Staple gun and staples (Only the TEACHER should staple things!)
- Scissors

Each group should draw out puppets in pencil on the large cardboard first then retrace and color with markers. Staple the large puppets to the 4-foot-tall pieces of wood leaving about one foot as a handle. Wrap the handle with duct tape to prevent splinters. Draw the smaller puppets on the white cardboard and color them in with markers or pencils. Cut out the smaller puppets. If the group has any time left over, they should practice with the puppets.

Practicing with the puppets can be difficult if they are so large that they bump the ceilings. We didn't have any trouble because we had high ceilings and good weather for practicing outside. You may want to refine the size of the puppets to be able to practice in your classroom space. We had some groups practice outside. The Lower School students were really in awe of the giant puppets as they watched the kids practice outside. At noon, we broke for lunch.

After lunch, we met in the auditorium to give a progress report to the entire Middle School. Each group should have a spokesperson assigned to do this. Having a time to share the progress of each group is important. The kids were really motivated for the afternoon activities after they heard other groups talk about their stories and their puppets.

The CBD groups then returned to their classrooms for an hour to finish coloring, stapling, and so on. Then they cleaned up.

The next activity is to rehearse with the puppets and refine the script. We allowed each group to use one half of the stage space. The reason only half the stage was used is that two groups could set up and then run their plays, one after another. Then we struck the stage and set up for two more plays. It really helped everything run smoothly. We also told the students to block everything downstage, that is, as close to the audience as possible because in our theater it is easier to hear when the performers are closer to the audience.

We also agreed that the performance should follow this outline:

1) Music introduces the show
2) The show
3) Music to signal the end of the show

Each group should have divided up the "parts" already. They need someone to run the music at the beginning and at the end of the show, people to play found-object instruments (the Band), people to manipulate the puppets (large and small), and a narrator. Sometimes there are really shy students who would rather run the music or play an instrument than appear onstage. Being sensitive to the needs of every student is important. Encourage the students to find a role that suits them.

Usually a group will get in two or three rehearsals before we return to the auditorium with our found-object instrument. You should watch the rehearsals and offer comments so that the students can refine their script to make it more cohesive and clear. The puppeteers should get used to manipulating the larger-than-life puppet. These rehearsals will be rough, but their purpose is to show the students where the holes are in the script. Revising the story now, before adding the music, is very important.

THE FOUND-OBJECT INSTRUMENTS

The first thing we did when everyone returned to the auditorium was to watch a video called *Robotique*. In this video, machines put a car together to music accompanied by "found" sound. After watching the video, we had a general discussion about how this wordless film still communicated ideas to us. We agreed that the music and found sounds were the key to creating the mood and enhancing the theme.

At this point the music teacher took over and demonstrated how many different sounds you can get from a simple object. Then she asked for three volunteers and their instruments. We played a bit of the video again with the sound turned down and the student volunteers enhanced the movie with their own sounds. The music teacher answered any questions that the students had about how to make unique and interesting sounds from the objects that they brought from home. Then the students were asked to return to their classrooms to experiment with their instruments and to incorporate these sounds into their plays.

The rehearsals with the instruments were noisy, but fun. The students began with a read-through of their script and sound was added as they went along. The percussive noises shouldn't detract from the storytelling, and you will just have to make some judgment calls on this. Some of the found instruments will be more effective than others, so after running through the script twice, ask the kids which sounds they want to keep and which ones they want to eliminate. With more rehearsal, they can refine the amount of noise and use the instruments to help the story along. The band members should mark their scripts with the music cues. Then the found-object instruments are handed over to the Band for a run-through of the entire play, complete with puppets and the opening and closing music from the tape.

At the end of this day your performance outline should look like this:

1) Music from tape as introduction
2) The story (enhanced with music from found objects)
3) Music to signal the end

DAY 3
REHEARSAL AND PERFORMANCE

We met in the auditorium to review the schedule for this exciting day. The CBD groups move to their classrooms to rehearse for about forty-five minutes. The students will probably need this time to practice with the Band of found-object instruments since they didn't have a lot of time to practice on the previous day.

The next step was to allow the groups to practice onstage. We came up with a way to give the groups rehearsal time that was less chaotic by developing an order of rotation and by pairing the groups up for this rotation. Only two groups could rehearse at a time in the auditorium. The other groups would work on activities that took place around the campus, such as continuing the growing chalk mural, playing outdoor games, and doing improvisational games in their classrooms. I stayed in the auditorium all day running the rehearsals while my colleagues helped run the other activities. Many of the groups opted to get in some extra rehearsals in their rooms. I left this choice up to the teachers that had been working and rehearsing with their groups. At any one time four groups were either in rehearsal, drawing with chalk, or playing games outside; and two groups were in the auditorium with me rehearsing. It was ordered chaos and it worked!

For the rehearsal in the auditorium to go smoothly, there must be absolute silence during rehearsal. One CBD group watches a show while the other performs. The watchers should be able to give some helpful praise and hints for improvements. The "performers" should set up the stage in silence, get to their places, and be ready to begin as soon as you give them the signal. The rehearsal time was fifteen minutes for each group. We had time slots scheduled as follows:

   9:30–10:00 then groups rotate
10:05–10:35 groups rotate
10:40–11:10 groups rotate
11:15–11:45 groups go to lunch

After lunch, the students returned to the auditorium for their setup. The performance order was the same as the morning rehearsal schedule.

OUR FINAL PERFORMANCE FOR
AN INVITED AUDIENCE

There was a great deal of excitement as the students prepared to present their shows to the lower school. Parents were also invited to the performance. The video teacher taped each show for watching at a future time. After the shows, we had refreshments and cleanup time.

We *all* enjoyed the performances: teachers, administrators, students, and parents! It was a huge group effort, and it built community in a way that had never been tried before. The students who were a part of this experience still remember it vividly. The theme was a positive look at the future and convinced us that the arts are a vital part of that future.

In the words of one of the teachers who led a CBD group,

Developing a unifying theme through interpretive drama with the giant puppets as a community-building project provided an outlet for each child to develop a persona that expressed his or her feelings in a safe and collaborative environment. The children worked together for a common, valid purpose and were able to bring their efforts together in a meaningful project that provided satisfying results to the community as a whole. It was a genuine experience for the students on many levels. The best part about it? They really enjoyed themselves and still speak of the experience to this day.

Ms. Riffle, middle school science

Getting a Bad Case of "Middle Mania"

In the introduction to this book I explain the reasons for trying a different approach to teaching drama in middle school. A diet of production after production dulls the imagination and sets up a hierarchy that prompts questions like, "Who has the lead?" But as I wrote and rewrote these chapters, I discovered another reason for trying something different in drama. The excitement is contagious!

Middle Mania is aptly named. Whether you try to incorporate B.O.P. or Clan Drama or Giant Puppets into your program, your "drama diet" will be invigorated. The energy from these imaginative lessons will spill over into other disciplines and encourage connections with other teachers. "Middle Mania" will spread throughout your school. You might even try your own version of Community Building Days!

When I read through other drama books for ideas, I try to figure out how on earth I will ever make the exercises work in a classroom situation. It seems that some ideas for drama originate on paper and end up staying there. The drama projects in this book have been taught, refined, and retaught in a classroom with real middle school students. They can be refined and stretched to meet your particular classroom needs. They WORK!

Not only do they work: These lessons are remembered year after year.

My Upper School students watch the Giant Puppet Show or the Clan Drama in rehearsal and remember their experiences in a highly positive way. Drama alums return to the school and catch a class doing the White Sock Puppet Monologue and recall how much fun they had with the B.O.P. project. Musical Chairs, Rock 'n' Roll Playwriting, Mask/ Movement live on in the memories of my students. Some of them still have the masks they wore!

The excitement is contagious and spreads to the parents, too. Every time we have a curriculum night at our school, parents tell me how much they would enjoy doing these imaginative projects. They never had the opportunity to take a drama class. They often offer to help on projects joining in on the fun and learning.

Throughout the year, my students share their enthusiasm for drama with a wide variety of audiences. Those audiences would remark on how much self-confidence and energy the youngsters had onstage and how much fun they were having during their performance. "Middle Mania" begins with you and the students, spreads to other teachers and parents, and reaches out to an appreciative audience.

My hope is that this book will not be one of those that sit on your shelf. I hope that it becomes dog-eared, refusing to stay closed on your desk. I want you to teach these lessons and adapt and change them and then e-mail me to let me know how they worked. My e-mail address is PMWIZARDJ@aol.com. I want you to get a bad case of "Middle Mania" and spread it around.

— Maureen Brady Johnson

Curriculum Summaries

DRAMA GRADE 6

Goal: Getting "Behind" Drama

Projects:
B.O.P. (Bag of Puppets), Mask/Movement, Speech, "Musical Chairs," Improvisation, Radio Plays

Overview:
The sixth grade year is the year that I begin to build a basis of trust and community. The program attempts to balance performance with process, that is, trying to be especially sensitive to the needs of each group. The Puppet Show and Mask/Movement are designed to keep the actors hidden so that they feel free to relax, risk, and perform onstage. Every project is designed to develop dramatic skills (life skills!), while boosting fragile self-confidence.

Content Area and Skills:
1. To develop a strong sense of trust and security onstage.
2. To allow students to take a variety of risks onstage.
3. To encourage creativity, group dynamics, decision making and self-reflection throughout the year
4. To challenge their stage ability and to help them grow as individuals
5. To increase self-awareness and self-confidence

Please see Grade Assessment Chart for skill development in each project.

Materials and Resources:
Puppets; white socks; half-face masks; large, oversized masks; music

DRAMA GRADE 7

Goal: Getting to the Root of Drama

Projects:
First quarter: Clan experience
Second quarter: Storytelling and Giant Puppet Shows
Third quarter: Speech
Fourth quarter: "Musical Chairs" and Improvisation.

Overview:
During the seventh grade year in drama, the history and origin of theater is explored. The Clan Drama experience begins the year. Students learn through the construction of an original play that drama began as people's attempt to explain the universe around them and to give them some control over it. Storytelling, an ancient dramatic form, is explored and used as a basis for a giant puppet show. Tapping into the dreams of the students, a unit on speech follows. Taking their own works from language arts class, a production called "Musical Chairs" gives the students an opportunity to perform their own pieces.

Skill Development:
See the Grade Assessment Chart for skills in process and production for each project.

Materials and Equipment:
Costumes; large puppet materials such as cardboard, 2–4 boards, paints, staple guns, carpet knives, etc; storybooks; student's original writings

Methodology:
Short lecture
Cooperative learning
Discussion
Problem solving

Individual assignments
Writing assignments
Dramatic production
Artistic renderings—costumes and props
Improvisational games

Assessment:
A cumulative record (grade assessment chart and comments) done quarter by quarter that shows the student's growth throughout the year

Short quizzes:
Observation by peers
Teacher and peer evaluation of process
Performances
Self-evaluation (use of videotape)

DRAMA GRADE 8
Goal: Putting it All Together in Middle School Drama

Projects:
First and Second Quarter: Play production
Third Quarter: Rock and Roll Playwriting
Fourth Quarter: Speech and Improvisation

Overview:
For the first two quarters, the 8th grade explores play production in depth. From the initial read through, to auditions, to blocking, to dress rehearsal, to final performance, a play is produced for classmates and parents. Makeup and costuming units of study support the students' background needed for a polished performance.

During the third quarter a unit on musical theater and the Rock and Roll playwriting experience culminates in a performance at the Spring Concert.

Fourth quarter emphasizes improvisational games and creative thinking in Drama. There will also be a unit on Speech with a variety of short and long speech-making assignments.

Materials and Equipment:
Scripts, costumes, make-up, props, set pieces, and the students themselves!

Methodology:
Short lecture
Rehearsal/dramatic production process
Cooperative learning
Discussion
Problem-solving
Artistic rendering of costumes and props
Improvisational games
Integration with music

Assessment:
- A cumulative record consisting of a grade assessment sheet and comments.
- Observation in class and during rehearsal by peers and teacher.
- Peer evaluation of process and performance.
- Self-evaluation through the use of videotaping.

Assignment Sheets

B.O.P (BAG OF PUPPETS)

B.O.P. ASSIGNMENTS

Students will receive a bag of puppets and write a puppet show consisting of three scenes that utilize all of the puppets. In addition to the script, the students will be responsible for a short descriptive paragraph of the setting of each scene, a short description of each character, and a detailed explanation of the plot (including the lesson that the characters learn in the play).

B.O.P. 1: Due at the end of class:
- Names of characters
- Character description (rough draft)
- The lesson learned
- Where the three scenes take place
- Rough outline of the action of the three scenes

B.O.P. 2: Due at the end of class:
- Rough draft of scene 1

B.O.P. 3: Due at the end of class:
- Rough draft of scenes 2 and 3

B.O.P. 4: Due at the beginning of class:
- Good copy of the script due to the teacher and group members
- Rehearsal of the play with the puppets during class time

B.O.P. 5: Rehearsal
- Use this class to refine and polish your script

B.O.P. 6: Performance (videotaped)

B.O.P. REFLECTION SHEET

Please answer these questions immediately after you watch a puppet performance. There are three class performances to see. Number the comments 1, 2, and 3 to correspond to the shows. Thank you.

Was the story line clear and easy to follow? Explain.
    1.

    2.

    3.

Were the relationships between the puppets clearly defined? Did the puppets come alive as characters?
    1.

    2.

    3.

What was the moral to the story?
    1.

    2.

    3.

Did the performance run smoothly? Were the puppeteers adept at handling the puppets?
    1.

    2.

    3.

Did the group project and enunciate?

1.

2.

3.

Which puppet show was your favorite and why?

1.

2.

3.

What would you change about the B.O.P. project if you were to do it again? Be honest with your answers. I use your suggestions to improve the project for the next group of students. Thank you.

B.O.P. SELF-ASSESSMENT

Please rate your group on the way that you worked together during this project. Use the scale of 1 through 5, 1 being the best rating and 5 being the lowest rating. Use the comments section to write a few sentences about the process.

Process _____

Creativity in approach _____

Deadlines met _____

Co-operative attitude _____

Working dynamics _____

Individual contributions _____

Leadership ability _____

Neatness _____

Attention to detail _____

Comments:

As you watch the puppet shows, use this part of the sheet to evaluate the performance. Use the same ratings as above and write a few sentences about the performance in the Comments section.

Performance _____

Projection _____

Enunciation _____

Dramatization _____

Puppet handling _____

Characterization _____

Self-confidence _____

Enthusiasm _____

Originality of script _____

Script construction and cohesiveness _____

Comments:

MASK/MOVEMENT

NOTES ON MYSELF
Please write complete responses to the questions that follow. Provide specific, concrete answers. You can imagine this as a section of your writing journal in which you are collecting information about yourself for future writing. If you draw a blank on a particular question, move ahead to others and return to the blank one(s) if you have time. Use the back side or another sheet if necessary.

1. What is my greatest fear?

2. What kinds of things do I dream when I sleep? (If you have a recurrent dream, describe it. Be as specific and concrete as possible.)

3. What is my first memory? How does it affect my life?

4. What is my favorite possession? Why?

5. Something I want but am afraid to ask for is:

6. What is my most distinctive physical characteristic and how would I describe it?

7. I need...

8. If I were an animal, what would I be?

9. If I were an object or tool, what would I be?

10. If I were a color, what would I be?

11. What time of day would I be?

12. If I were a plant or a tree, what would I be?

13. If I were to write a book, what would its title be?

14. What is the most difficult thing I've ever done?

15. What is one thing I want to do or be before my life is over?

16. What is one thing I would change about my life up to now?

17. What is one thing I would never change about my life up to now?

MASK/MOVEMENT

This is a student-generated list given to me by Matt Vanek to help with the improvisations and the Mask/Movement project.

EMOTIONS AND CHARACTER TRAITS:

Nervous	Neat
Happy	Persuasive
Sad	Pensive
Flirty	Timid
Sassy	Psychic
Tense	Angry
Excitable	Sloppy
Ironic	Questioning
Strong-willed	Quibbling
Weak-willed	Irrational
Hateful/Spiteful	Idiotic
Bored	Obedient
Shocked	Oaf-like
Exhausted	Cold-blooded
Ecstatic	Ruthless
Overwhelmed	Joyful
Depressed	Interfering
Frustrated	Accident-prone
Frightened	Intense
Jealous	Confused
Love struck	Curious
Spontaneous	Patient
Hopeful	Persistent
Pessimistic	Lying
Suave	Charismatic
Serene	Outspoken
Paranoid	Obnoxious
Sneaky	Sad
Suspicious	Whining
Rude	Sincere
Witty	Bungling
Compassionate	Sleepy
Conceited	Lazy
Shy	

CLAN DRAMA: SOLVING A MYSTERY

CLAN DRAMA ASSIGNMENTS

Classes 1 and 2: Due at the end of the first and second class:

- The name of your tribe
- A short essay (rough draft) with at least five paragraphs describing the place that you live and your way of life. This should be a detailed description that includes the entire habitat (flora and fauna), the types of dwellings that you live in, and how you survive in this habitat.
- An artistic rendering of the symbol of your clan (rough draft)
- A short essay (several paragraphs) summarizing the action and plot of the story
- A list of characters, each with a short description, i.e., Trog…a slow-moving, dim-witted cave man with a heart of gold

Class 3: Final copies (perfect drafts) of all of the above. A rough draft of the first two scenes is due at the end of class. (Remember: The entire play should be five minutes long.)

Class 4: A rough draft of the entire play is due (four scenes).

Class 5: Final drafts (perfect copies) are due at the beginning of class. There should be enough copies for every performer and one for the teacher.

Classes 5 and 6: Rehearsal. Check the running time and make the necessary changes to the script.

Class 7: Bring in costumes, props, construct the symbol. Any time left over should be used for rehearsal.

Class 8: Dress rehearsal with costumes, props, and symbol.

Classes 9 and 10: Performance and videotaping.

Grades are based on two major areas: paperwork and performance. Deadlines must be met. If someone is absent, you are still responsible for the paperwork due. Make sure you have a backup system in place to cover occurrences such as this. Five minutes before class ends someone from each group should report in to me on the deadlines and paperwork that is due. Performance will be graded on stage presence, creativity of the script, smoothness of presentation. You will also be graded on your ability to work well in a group. Your clan members will also grade you on these points.

CLAN DRAMA: VIDEO VIEWING FORM

On a separate sheet of paper:

- List the titles of the Clan Dramas and their themes.

- Which Clan Drama did you enjoy the most?

- List five things that the performers did to make the drama enjoyable.

- What did you learn from the other Clan Dramas that you might have done to improve your own production?

- How did you feel when you were performing in front of everyone else?

- How did you feel when you were watching the video of your performance? ...when you watched the other clans performing?

- Why do you think we did this project? What did you learn about theater that you didn't know before?

- What grade do you think you deserve and why?

- What grade do the other members of your Clan deserve and why?

CLAN DRAMA: TIME OUT FOR REFLECTION

Name_____

1) Has your group constructed a clear, explanatory play about the mystery of nature that you received? Give a short summary of how you arrived at the final production.

2) Comment on each person's cooperative attitude and give them the grade you think that they deserve. Do the same for yourself. Did you present solutions instead of roadblocks? Did you compromise? Did you meet all of the deadlines?

NAME:_____ Grade_____

NAME:_____ Grade_____

NAME:_____ Grade_____

NAME:_____ Grade_____

Grade Assessment
Charts

DRAMA ASSESSMENT CHART

"B.O.P." (Bag of Puppets)

Name_____Grade_____

Advisor_____Date_____

Ratings are: Fair, Satisfactory, or Excellent

Process:

Creativity in approach _____

Originality of script _____

Script construction and cohesiveness _____

Deadlines met _____

Cooperative attitude _____

Working dynamics _____

Individual contributions _____

Leadership ability _____

Neatness _____

Attention to detail _____

Performance

Projection _____

Enunciation _____

Dramatization _____

Puppet handling _____

Characterization _____

Self-confidence _____

Enthusiasm _____

Comments:

DRAMA ASSESSMENT CHART
Mask/Movement

Name_____Grade_____

Advisor_____Date_____

Ratings are: Fair, Satisfactory, or Excellent

Process:
    Ability to take direction   _____
    Cooperation   _____
    Deadlines met   _____
    Creativity of approach   _____
    Expressiveness   _____

Performance:
    Large body movement   _____
    Coordination   _____
    Sense of rhythm   _____

Comments:

DRAMA ASSESSMENT CHART

Clan Drama

Name_____Grade_____

Advisor_____Date_____

Ratings are: Fair, Satisfactory, or Excellent

Process:
    Understanding of dramatic form   _____
    Scene construction   _____
    Transitions   _____
    Cooperative attitude   _____
    Adaptability   _____
    Use of class time   _____
    Individual contribution   _____
    Creativity of approach   _____
    Deadlines met   _____

Performance:
    Performance quality   _____
    Attention to detail   _____
    Costuming   _____
    Enunciation   _____
    Projection   _____

Comments:

DRAMA ASSESSMENT CHART

Giant Puppet Show

Name_____Grade_____

Advisor_____Date_____

Ratings are: Fair, Satisfactory, or Excellent

Process:
    Carryover (classroom to stage)   _____
    Ability to take direction   _____
    Use of rehearsal time   _____
    Cooperation   _____

Performance: (Storytelling)
    Facial expressiveness   _____
    Vocal expressiveness   _____

Performance: (Giant Puppets)
    Ability to handle puppets   _____
    Large stage movement   _____
    Small stage movement   _____
    Cleanup   _____

Comments:

DRAMA ASSESSMENT CHART

"Musical Chairs"

Name_____Grade_____

Advisor_____Date_____

Ratings are: Fair, Satisfactory, or Excellent

Process:
    Choice of piece   _____
    Ability to take direction   _____
    Creative/inventive attitude   _____

Performance:
    Creativity in movement   _____
    Performance of movement   _____
    Spirit of cooperation   _____
    Self-confidence   _____
    Enunciation   _____
    Projection   _____
    Dramatic quality of performance   _____

Comments:

DRAMA ASSESSMENT CHART
Rock 'n' Roll Playwriting

Name_____Grade_____

Advisor_____Date_____

Ratings are: Fair, Satisfactory, or Excellent

Process:

    Understanding basic musical theater concepts

    Deadlines met

    Cooperative attitude

    Use of class time

    Line memorization

    Song memorization

    Blocking memorization

Performance:

    Enthusiasm on stage

    Expressiveness in body movement

    Expressiveness with voice

    Focus and concentration

Reflections on *Middle Mania* projects

Chapter One: B.O.P.

"The innovative use of puppetry in this unit allows students the opportunity to fully express themselves artistically, verbally and dramatically."

—Rachelle Bilz, parent of a student participant

"The videotape of our puppet show was almost worn out at our house, we played it so much. I loved B.O.P."

—Julia Bilz, student participant

"To start from the chaos of a bag of seemingly unrelated puppets and end up with a polished performance... It's hilarious. It's crazy. It's fun."

—Jake, student participant

Chapter Two: Mask/Movement

"It was a chilly Halloween night, and the Trick-or-Treaters were not at all as cheerful as they had been earlier that night while energetically knocking on doors. Presently, the Trick-or-Treating trio was anxiously walking through a graveyard, clutching their flashlights and pumpkins with white knuckles. Their fears were not unfounded, for everyone knows that walking through a graveyard on Halloween night is an invitation for danger. Without fail, the graveyard came to life, so to speak. The Zombies began to advance toward the three girls, undeterred by swinging pumpkins and waving flashlights. Nothing could save the girls... nothing except Super Josh! In the knick of time Super Josh arrived, battled the Zombies, and saved the terrified Trick-or-Treaters. Even though it's years later, I still remember the fun we had doing the Mask/Movement project!"

—Supriya, student participant

"The thing I like about the lessons which you have designed for middle school is that they are sensitive to the developmental level of your students. The sixth grade "Mask/Movement" project, for example, provides time for kids to get comfortable on stage by allowing them to "hide" while still performing. The emotional qualities of the mask also give the student solid, understandable characteristics to explore and develop onstage.

In this way, students begin to develop the tools of an actor, while still using concepts which are within their daily experience. They are able to act without becoming lost or nervous."

— Matt Vanek, art teacher

Chapter Three: Clan Drama

"The clan drama experience helped me realize the importance of cooperation in a group. There were classes where we couldn't agree on anything. But as soon as we were willing to cooperate, the clan drama started to come together and we had a really good time."

—E.B. seventh grade student

"It's a lot of work putting a production together. We had to write the scenes, block the play, find costumes and props, and work together to meet the deadlines. But we were really proud of the final product. Our clan was the best."

—Marissa seventh grade student

Chapter Four: Giant Puppet Show

"I thought that the giant puppet show project was really cool because it showed us that we could act without using our faces!"

—Catherine, student participant

"The Giant Puppet show gave kids who were afraid to be onstage a chance to act and hide behind something. They weren't afraid anymore."

—Juliet, student participant

Chapter Five: "Musical Chairs"

"I didn't think that my poem about the fruit floating in the Jell-O was very funny. But when I performed the poem in front of an audience, they laughed. I felt good about that."

—Saran, student participant

"I remember we did our funky walk to 'Octopus' Garden.' I wasn't afraid to go onstage because we practiced so much and everyone else was having such a good time that I did, too."

—Sean, student participant

Chapter Six: Rock 'n' Roll Playwriting

"My music students love the 'oldies'. Adding drama and giving them a chance to perform these classic songs was wonderful."

—Mrs. Crooker, music teacher

"This project carried the songs of the 50s one step further by imagining a before and after to each heart-rending tune. I loved watching the students appreciate the songs that I grew up with."

—Mark, father of a student performer

"The best part about the Playwriting/Musical workshop was the fact that for a week AFTER the show the high schoolers were telling US how much they liked the show."

—Donald, student participant

Chapter Seven: Community Building Days

"Ms. Riffle asked us about our ideas about the future of the Earth. I said, 'The earth will be filled with chameleons. People-sized chameleons. The future is all about quick changes. Chameleons are always changing with their environment.' So we made a huge chameleon puppet to illustrate our story about the future."

—Ian, student participant

"Developing a unifying theme through interpretive drama with the Giant puppets as a community building project provided an outlet for each child to develop a persona that expressed their feelings in a safe and collaborative environment. The children worked together for a common, valid purpose and were able to bring their efforts together in a meaningful project that provided satisfying results to the community as a whole. It was a genuine experience for the students on many levels. The best part about it? They really enjoyed themselves and still speak of the experience to this day."

—Ms. Riffle, middle school science teacher

"Your book sounds wonderful. And I'm not one bit surprised that you've been asked to write it. I can't wait to read it. And you can be darn sure I'll recommend it to everyone I know. I'm happy to offer a thought on community building, though I'm afraid I won't come close to doing justice to the various projects—or to your pedagogy. And while it is true that I was the division for some of your work, the work stood on its own. You could have placed a stone in my office, and your ideas would have flourished. What makes you the genius that you are is that you know about that magic space where early adolescents and drama meet—that land of "what if" where these people who aren't quite children yet aren't quite teenagers can figure out how to become the people they need to be. I'm proud to say I've always stood in awe of your brilliance as a teacher. That you're having a book published is simply confirmation of what those of us who have been lucky enough to work with you know only too well: You work magic in the classroom and onstage."

—Dr. Michael Ebeling